Simple
Sermons
for
today's
world

The "Simple Sermon" series by W. Herschel Ford . . .

Seven Simple Sermons on the Saviour's Last Words
Seven Simple Sermons on the Second Coming
Simple Sermons About Jesus Christ
Simple Sermons for a Sinful Age
Simple Sermons for Funeral Services
Simple Sermons for Midweek Services
Simple Sermons for Saints and Sinners
Simple Sermons for Special Days and Occasions
Simple Sermons for Sunday Evening
Simple Sermons for Sunday Morning
Simple Sermons for Time and Eternity
Simple Sermons for Times Like These
Simple Sermons for Today's World
Simple Sermons for 20th Century Christians
Simple Sermons on Conversion and Commitment
Simple Sermons From the Book of Acts
Simple Sermons From the Gospel of John
Simple Sermons From the Gospel of Matthew
Simple Sermons on Evangelistic Themes
Simple Sermons on Heaven, Hell and Judgment
Simple Sermons on Prayer
Simple Sermons on Prophetic Themes
Simple Sermons on Salvation and Service
Simple Sermons on Simple Themes
Simple Sermons on the Christian Life
Simple Sermons on Great Christian Doctrines
Simple Sermons on the Old-Time Religion
Simple Sermons on the Seven Churches of Revelation
Simple Sermons on the Ten Commandments
Simple Talks for Christian Workers
Simple Sermons on Life and Living
Simple Sermons for Modern Man
Simple Sermons on Old Testament Texts
Simple Sermons on New Testament Texts
Simple Sermons for a World in Crisis
Simple Sermons on Grace and Glory

Simple Sermons for today's world

by
W. HERSCHEL FORD, B.A., D.D.

Introduction by
Dr. W. Ramsey Pollard
Former President, Southern Baptist Convention

ZONDERVAN
PUBLISHING HOUSE
OF THE ZONDERVAN CORPORATION | GRAND RAPIDS, MICHIGAN 49506

SIMPLE SERMONS FOR TODAY'S WORLD
Copyright © 1960 by Zondervan Publishing House
Grand Rapids, Michigan

Sixteenth printing   1979
ISBN 0-310-24721-7

Printed in the United States of America

*This book is dedicated to the fine
people on the Staff of the
First Baptist Church
El Paso, Texas
faithful friends who helped me greatly
in the work of the Lord*

INTRODUCTION

Dr. Ford has given us his best in *Simple Sermons for Today's World*. His successful ministry is understood when his sermons are read. He speaks to the hearts and minds of his congregation. Solid scholarship and fervent evangelism are happily combined. The illustrations are superb. I heartily commend his latest book. It will be a source of blessing to many thousands of God's children.

W. RAMSEY POLLARD, D.D.
Pastor, Bellevue Baptist Church
Memphis, Tennessee, and
Former President, Southern Baptist Convention

CONTENTS

1. The Greatest Personality in the Bible............ 13
   Philippians 2:1-11
2. The Riches of the Redeemed (Part One)........ 22
   Romans 8:1
3. The Riches of the Redeemed (Part Two)........ 30
   Romans 8:28
4. The Riches of the Redeemed (Part Three)....... 38
   Romans 8:35-39
5. The Sweetest Name I Know.................... 45
   Philippians 2:5-11
6. My God and I............................... 56
   Matthew 6:33
7. Who's That Knocking at My Heart's Door?....... 67
   Revelation 3:20
8. Paul's Knows 76
   II Timothy 1:12; Romans 8:28; II Corinthians 5:1
9. The End of the Trail (Part One)................ 86
   II Timothy 4:6-8
10. The End of the Trail (Part Two)................ 95
    II Timothy 4:6-8
11. The Greatest Visit Ever Made..................104
    John 1:1-13
12. The Voice of Jesus 111
    John 7:40-46

Simple Sermons for today's world

Sermon 1

THE GREATEST PERSONALITY IN THE BIBLE

Philippians 2:1-11

We are more interested in personalities than in principles. People themselves always interest us more than any of the world's great teachings. For instance, sometime ago I picked up a magazine which contained two articles about Cuba. One article spoke of the economics and politics of the island, the other article spoke of the personal life of the Cuban leader, Fidel Castro. I immediately passed over the article which spoke of the economics and politics of Cuba and began to read about the dynamic leader who overthrew the Batista regime. It is the same way with the Bible. Some parts of the Word of God teach us principles and doctrines, such as the Book of Romans. Now these parts of the Bible are very important. We ought to read them and study them and live by them. But it is more exciting to read about Joseph and his trials and triumphs, about David killing Goliath and about the thrilling conversion of Paul.

Now as we think of great personalities let us ask the question, "Who is the greatest personality in the Bible?" It is not Moses. He was a mighty man, the greatest man of the Old Testament. God called him to lead Israel to the Promised Land. He overcame Pharaoh and led over two and a half million slaves to freedom. At Sinai he received the Law and the Ten Commandments. When he died God Himself buried him. Yet Moses was not the greatest personality in the Bible.

It is not David. He was a great sinner and a great saint. He was "a man after God's own heart." His life was filled with wondrous deeds. He wrote most of the Psalms in the Bible. You can't beat him when you hear him saying, "The Lord is my Shepherd, I shall not want." Yet he was not the greatest personality in the Bible. It was not John the Baptist. He was a mighty preacher, he baptized the Lord Jesus Christ. He didn't have to advertise to get a crowd. He preached on the banks of the River Jordan, the cities emptied themselves and the people came out to hear him. His preaching brought results, thousands repented of their sins and were baptized. Jesus said that no greater man had come into the world. Yet John the Baptist was not the greatest personality in the Bible.

It is not Simon Peter. He was a simple fisherman, but God called him to be the preacher at Pentecost. Three thousand people were converted that day. We are interested in Peter because he was so human, he was so much like the rest of us. One day he was on the mountain top and the next day he was down in the valley. One day he was swearing allegiance to Christ, the next day he was swearing that he never knew Him. He was a great man. God used him in spite of his human frailties. But he was not the greatest personality in the Bible.

It is not the Apostle Paul. He was God's biggest man this side of the Lord Jesus Christ. He was a dynamic, forceful, vigorous leader. He wrote most of the New Testament. He has influenced the thinking of the world more than any man except his Master. Yet Paul was not the greatest personality in the Bible.

Jesus Christ is the greatest personality of the Bible and of all the ages. His Name as such is not mentioned in the Old Testament, yet every part of the Old Testament points to him in some way. When we think of Moses, the deliverer, we think of Christ who delivered us from sin. When we think of the manna in the wilderness, we remember

The Greatest Personality in the Bible 15

that Jesus is the Bread from heaven. When we think of the blood of the Passover Lamb, we remember that Jesus is the Lamb of God. When we think of Joshua leading Israel to the Promised Land, we think of Christ leading us to heaven. When we think of Abraham tying Isaac to the sacrificial altar, we remember that Jesus was nailed to the cross. When we think of the rock giving water in the wilderness, we remember Jesus, the Rock of Ages, giving us the Water of Life. Yes, Jesus is the heart of the Old Testament.

Then when we come to the New Testament we see Him filling every page. If we were to give a new title to the New Testament, it would be, "All About Jesus." Now let us look into the Bible and see "Jesus only."

I. He Was the Prophesied Messiah

Go with me to the Garden of Eden. Adam and Eve have just committed the first sin. Now they stand before God. Satan is there in the form of a serpent. And God Himself pronounces a curse upon Satan. In Genesis 3:15 he says, "And I will put enmity between thee and the woman, and between thy seed and her seed; it shall bruise thy head, and thou shalt bruise his heel."

God right here is predicting that Christ, the seed of the woman, will be bruised by Satan. This happened when He died upon Calvary. God also predicted that Christ would crush the head of Satan. This will happen at the end of the age when Jesus takes over. This then was the first prophecy of the coming Messiah.

Now listen to the greatest prophecy in the Old Testament, Isaiah 53:5, 6, "But he was wounded for our transgressions, he was bruised for our iniquities: the chastisement of our peace was upon him; and with his stripes we are healed. All we like sheep have gone astray; we have turned every one to his own way; and the Lord hath laid on him the iniquity of us all."

A preacher friend of mine was talking to a Jew who was well versed in the Old Testament Scriptures. He asked him this question, "Who was the prophet Isaiah talking about?"

And the Jew answered, "I do not know."

But we know that he is talking about Jesus. Hundreds of years before Christ was born, God spoke through His prophets. He told where the Messiah would be born, how He would be born, how He would live, how He would die, how He would be buried.

Suppose that I wrote an article about a man coming to our city. Suppose that I told you how he would arrive, how he would be dressed, and how he would act. Then suppose that one month later you saw this man arrive in the way that I predicted. Suppose that he looked and dressed and acted as I said he would. Certainly then you would say, "This is the man he was writing about." Well, these prophets seven hundred years before Christ told about the coming Messiah. When He came those who knew the prophecies cried out, "This is He of whom the prophets spoke."

A church was started in a very exclusive section of a city. On Sunday mornings the cars were noisy as the members drove up to the church. The people in the church sang the old hymns so vigorously that they could be heard for a half block. A Gentile man got up a petition to put the church out of that area. Those who were out late on Saturday night wanted to sleep on Sunday morning. When they asked a Jew in the neighborhood to sign, he said, "No, I will not sign that petition. Those people sing as if they believed that the Messiah had come. If I believed it, I would shout it from every housetop."

Well, we know that Jesus has come. He fulfilled all the Old Testament prophecies. He was the prophesied Messiah.

II. He Was the Rejected Saviour

John tells us that "he came unto his own and his own received him not." Can you imagine the heartbreak which this rejection brought to Christ? The people had looked forward to His coming. They had sung about it. They had talked about it, they had prayed about it. But when He came they did not receive Him. This must have hurt the tender heart of the Saviour. We know more about Christ than those people did. We have the Bible to tell us all about Him. We live two thousand years this side of the cross. We have seen His influence upon human history. Surely only a foolish man would reject Him now. Yet there are many who do this very thing. Today He lays claim to your allegiance. He knocks at the door of your heart. He wants to be your Lord as well as your Saviour. If you do not give Him the rightful place in your heart, you have as truly rejected Him as did these men of old.

One day He said, "You will not come unto me that ye might have life." He wants us to have everlasting life, so He offers Himself to us as a Saviour. He wants us to have the abundant life here, so He offers Himself to us as Lord.

III. He Was the Crucified Redeemer

"While we were yet sinners, Christ died for our sins." Go with me today to Calvary. Christ had spent the night in humiliation and suffering. They had beaten Him until the blood ran down His back to the pavement. They had pressed the crown of thorns upon His brow. They had marched Him out to the edge of the city between rows of howling sinners. Now as they lay Him upon the cross and you hear the ringing blows of the hammer, they nail great spikes in His hands and feet. They lift the cross in the air and you hear a dull thud as it drops into the hole prepared for it. Jesus hangs there and bleeds His life away.

Oh, look, look, look, poor mortals! Why is He there? He hangs there because of our sin. He went to the cross to save us. He shed His blood in order to give us eternal life. What do you say as you see Him on that cross? Do you say, "It is nothing to me"? Do you say, "What has that to do with me"? Or do you say, "Oh, how I love Him. I am going to turn my back upon my sin and live only, always for Him"?

A mother asked her little boy what he would say if he could talk straight to God, and the little boy said, "I would ask Him to love me when I am naughty." And God did just that. When we were sinful, when we were far away from God, He loved us enough to die for us.

IV. He Was the Risen Lord

They sealed Him in a Roman tomb and planted soldiers to watch the grave. But in spite of all their precautions, Jesus got up out of that grave and marched away. The King of life could not be held by death. The Lord of heaven couldn't be kept in a grave. The Bible tells us that "because he arose, we, too, shall rise." His footsteps led down into the grave, but they led out on the other side. And though some day we may follow these steps down into the grave, because of faith in Him we will follow them out the other side and into the Land of Glory.

What is Jesus doing now? He is up in heaven interceding for us and waiting for the time to come when He will return to earth. We read that "He ever liveth to make intercession for us." Oh, it is wonderful to have Christ praying for us!

V. He Will Be Our Returning and Reigning King

Someday He is coming in the air. This first phase of His return is described in the Bible as His coming like a thief in the night. You may be at home, you may be asleep, you may be at work, you may be in church. If you are a child of God, He will find you and catch you up to meet Him in the air. If you die before that time, you will rise before those who are living upon the earth and you, too, will meet the Lord in the air.

Last summer I was in my home city of Atlanta, and went out to visit West View Cemetery. I stood by the cemetery lot which I purchased some years ago. As I looked upon that lot I said to myself, "If the Lord tarries it will not be long until I lie beneath this sod." I then went back to the cemetery office to get some information and told the secretary there my name. She then asked me the question, "Are you the Dr. W. Herschel Ford who wrote the book, *Seven Simple Sermons on the Second Coming?*" When I told her that I was she said, "We have a Bible Class on Tuesday mornings and we are studying your book on the Second Coming." We discussed this great truth a few minutes and when I turned to go, I said to her, "If Jesus comes soon, I will not need that cemetery lot."

Yes, in I Thessalonians Paul tells us that when Jesus comes in the air, He will gather up all of His children, dead or alive, give them new life and take them in glory into heaven. Yes, this is the first phase of the Lord's return. This is His coming for His saints.

Then later He is coming to earth with His saints to reign. The Bible describes this coming as being like a flash of lightning. Everyone will see it. Then He will reign upon the Throne of David. God has promised Him this privilege. No one reigns there now, but Christ will sit upon that throne. We call this period the millennium. This will be a thousand years of peace and plenty and prosperity. There will be no wars, for the nations will be under His control. There will be no poverty, for all of us will enjoy His riches. There will be no sorrow, no tears, no death. Not all those on the earth will be perfect, but He will reign with an iron hand and put down all sin and evil.

The matter of a reunion with our loved ones comes in right here. Our spirits go up to heaven when we die. Our bodies go up when Jesus comes in the air. It will not be a body like the one that is buried, but a body in His own likeness. During this time we will be united with our loved ones, but after all, this is not the most important thing. The most important thing is that we will see Jesus and be with Him.

A preacher in Denver recently heard that President Eisenhower was there visiting in his mother-in-law's modest home. He knew that the President would leave at a certain hour to go to the Air Force Academy. He joined the crowds in front of the home and waited to see the President. Telling about it later he said, "Several large cars were waiting in front of the home and the police were holding back the crowds. The eyes of everyone were upon the front door. The door soon opened and a little girl came out. She was the President's granddaughter. Then the President came out, waved his hand to the crowd and entered his car. The crowd applauded him. Who was with him? I don't know. Maybe his son, maybe his wife. If I saw them at all, it was out of the corner of my eyes. The President was the center of attention. He was the one whom I wanted to see."

People often ask me the question, "Do you think that I will know my husband, my father, my loved ones in heaven?" But no one ever asks the question, "Do you think I will know Jesus?" But when we get to heaven every eye will be centered upon Him. We will be so busy watching Him and rejoicing in His presence that everything else will fade into insignificance.

What is the practical application of these truths? Well, let us realize what a great Saviour we have. Let us thank Him for all that He has done, is doing and will do. Let us not leave Him outside the door of our hearts and lives. Let us be busy for Him. The question should not be, "When is He coming?" but, "Am I a good witness for Him?"

We can do two things. We can be busy for Him, yet always looking for Him. In the evening a wife prepares supper for her husband. She doesn't know the minute that he will be coming home. But she doesn't sit down, she is busy in the kitchen, yet she is listening for the sound of his key in the door. So must we be working, watching and waiting for Jesus.

Then let us remember that we are going to face Him someday. Will it be a time of joy or a time of sorrow? If you haven't lived for Him, you will cry out, "Lord, let me go back. Give me another chance." But then it will be too late. If you have lived for Him, you will not be ashamed and you will not be afraid. You will be glad to see Him and fall at His feet and thank Him for all that He has done for you.

The greatest personality in the Bible can become the greatest person in your life if you will only let Him have His way with you.

Sermon 2

THE RICHES OF THE REDEEMED
(PART ONE)

Romans 8:1

Christians are the richest people in the world. Non-Christians are the poorest. Go with me to a home on the edge of the city. The family living there has very little. The house is small, the furniture is cheap. But on the table is a Bible which shows evidence of being well-used. As the family sits down to a frugal meal we hear the voice of the father being lifted in thanksgiving to God. The spirit of Jesus Christ permeates this home, for all those in the family are Christians. They all love Christ and they are all growing in grace. When the Lord's Day comes, we see them on the way to church. When the offering plate passes by they put the Lord's money in it. It isn't much, but they know it belongs to the Lord and they give it to Him. When their pastor preaches they listen intently and rejoice that their names are written in heaven. When they see souls saved, they thank God that salvation has come to others. When the benediction is pronounced, they speak cordially to their Christian friends and start the homeward journey.

Look at them as they go. They don't ride in a big car, they don't wear expensive clothes. Yet I tell you that they are rich. They are rich in this world and rich for the next world. All the treasures in Christ are theirs. Now that's a picture of many families in our church. We have no millionaires in our church, but we are a rich church. We are rich in the things that count most. We are rich in the blessings of heaven.

But look into another house. We will not [...]
for if Christ doesn't dwell there, it isn't a h[ome...]
big house. Its floors are covered with the fine [...]
pensive pictures hang upon every wall. T[...]
are luxurious. Sterling silver is there, imp[...]
there. But when these people sit down to eat their sumptuous meals, no one looks to God in gratitude. No Scripture is ever read in this home and the Name of Jesus is never mentioned. These people ride in their big cars, but they don't go to God's house. They spend their money, but none goes into God's treasury. They wear fine clothes and expensive jewelry, but they don't have in their hearts the peace of God.

Look at these people. This is a picture of many families. They are rich, popular, well-educated. But in God's sight they are the poorest of the poor. They are going to live a little while and then die and leave all these things behind them. They are living for this world only, which means that they are committing suicide for the world to come. They had better enjoy what they have here, because there is nothing but hell and suffering awaiting them after death.

Thank God, you and I can be rich in Christ. The redeemed of the Lord are the richest people in all the world. Now as we turn to Romans 8 we hear Paul telling us three ways in which we are rich. First, he says that we have no condemnation, then he says that for us there is no complication, then he says that for the Christian there is no separation. No condemnation — no complication — no separation. Oh, what a trinity of riches for the redeemed! In this sermon let us think only of "No Condemnation." We see two things here in the text: the persons addressed and the promise given.

I. THE PERSONS ADDRESSED

Paul here tells us that he is speaking of those who are "in Christ Jesus." There is no condemnation for them.

But there are many who are not in Christ Jesus. What

does the Bible say about them? John 3:36: ". . . he that believeth not the Son shall not see life; but the wrath of God abideth on him." John 3:18: ". . . but he that believeth not is condemned already, because he hath not believed in the name of the only begotten Son of God."

Now suppose Paul had said only, "There is no condemnation." Then every sinner in the world would cry out, "That's fine, we are going along with Paul. It doesn't matter how we live or what we do, everything will work out all right in the end and we will all be together in heaven." Now that's what many people believe today. They say that God is such a great God of love that He will take them home at the end of the way, regardless of the fact that they have sinned and broken His laws and trampled His Son under foot. Surely we will agree that God is a God of love, but He is not going to let His love blot out His justice.

If God permitted the sinner to go unpunished, regardless of what he had done, even the sinner would lose respect for God. Suppose that you had murdered five people in cold blood, breaking the hearts of five loving wives and a number of helpless children. And suppose that when you came before the judge, he said, "I know you have committed an awful crime, but I am a loving judge. Go on home, you are free." You and all the world would lose respect for that judge. Well, if God said to every sinner in the world, "It doesn't matter how you have lived upon the earth, it doesn't matter how much you have sinned. There is nothing to it, just enter into heaven and enjoy the blessings of the redeemed" — if God said that He just wouldn't be God and no one would respect Him.

Now this is the serpent's gospel — to say that there is no punishment for sin. We remember the conversation in the Garden of Eden between Eve and the serpent. She told the serpent that God would send death upon her and Adam if they sinned. But Satan, in the guise of a serpent, said,

"You shall not surely die." It is simply a matter of God's word against Satan's word. God says, "The wages of sin is death." Satan says, "Go on in sin, nothing will happen to you."

So we see that some are condemned already and they will be forever lost, if they don't repent of their sins and come to Him who alone can save. What does a lost man have waiting for him? The Bible calls this a "fearful looking for of judgment and of fiery indignation." I would hate to stand where the sinner stands today and have to think that there is nothing to look forward to but death and hell. Yet that is all there is to a sinner's future.

Robert Murray M'Cheyne was a great preacher of Scotland. He died as a young man, but his name had become a household word in thousands of Scottish homes. He preached one night on the text, "I am the door, by me if any man enter in, he shall be saved." In the congregation there was a lost man to whom he had often preached and spoken to personally about his soul. That night the Holy Spirit shook that man in convicting power. He saw himself as a lost soul on the way to hell. He looked to Christ and was saved. He said to the preacher, "I got in tonight. I know I am saved. The trouble before is that I was trying to go in the wrong door."

"What do you mean?" asked the preacher.

And the man said, "I have been trying to get in at the saint's door. I thought that I had to live a perfect life to be saved, and I knew that I couldn't do it. You made it clear tonight that I must go in the sinner's door. I know Jesus is that door. So I have entered in, and thank God, a sinner has been saved." Oh, the world is filled with people who are trying to enter through the wrong door! They are condemned now and will be condemned forever. Why? Because they are not in Christ Jesus.

Now how does one get into Christ Jesus? Not by a good life, yet many are trying to get in that way. I talked to a man who told me that he lived a good life and expected that good life to take him to heaven. I handed him the Bible and said, "Show me where it says in God's Word, 'Live a good life and thou shalt be saved.'" Of couse, he couldn't do it. Neither are we saved by good works, yet millions of people are saying, "I will pile up my good works, then when God sees what I have done, He will take me to Himself." Yet the Bible tells us that we will never be saved by our works. Neither will we be saved by our gifts. If you gave a million dollars every day to the cause of Christ, that would not wash away a single sin. You should give because you are saved, but all your giving will not save you. Neither are we saved by baptism and church membership. You can be baptized in every stream in the world and join every church of every denomination and this will not carry you to heaven. Too many people today are depending upon their church membership to get them to heaven.

There is just one way to get into Jesus Christ. Ephesians 2:8 tells us that salvation is by grace through faith. There are two great words here — grace and faith. The "grace" is God's part. It means all the loving kindness of God extended to a lost sinner who has broken His laws and rejected His Son. God's grace is so marvelous and so wonderful that the human tongue can never describe it. The other word is "faith." That is man's part. It means to turn your back upon your sin and look up in faith toward the Son of God, fully trusting Him to save you.

Why do we make salvation so difficult to understand? Just throw aside all of your sins, all of your doubts, all of your human notions about salvation, and look up into His wonderful face in faith and He will save you. The Bible says, "Believe on the Lord Jesus Christ and thou shalt be saved." Jesus says, "Him that cometh to me, I will in no wise cast out." Jesus says, "I am the way, the truth and the life. No man cometh unto the Father but by me."

The Riches of the Redeemed (Part One)

There are many bridges over the Mississippi River, but only one bridge spans the chasm between a sinful man and a holy God, and that is Jesus. There are many roads from New York to Los Angeles, but there is only one road to heaven, and Jesus is that road. There are many ships that ply the waters from New York to London, but there is only one ship that will take you to heaven, and that is Jesus.

When Napoleon was in power, he wanted to bestow the cross of the French Legion of Honor upon Rosa Bonheur, the famous painter. But no woman had ever received this honor and Napoleon was afraid that popular opinion might condemn him for thus honoring a woman. So he left the imperial palace and left his wife, the Empress, as regent in his stead. One day, entirely unannounced, the empress went to see Rosa Bonheur. When the artist arose to receive the distinguished guest, the empress threw her arms around her and kissed her. Then after the empress left the artist discovered that, as her royal guest had kissed her, she had pinned the cross of the Legion of Honor upon her breast.

That is what Jesus does for us. When we rise up out of our sin and unbelief He throws His arms about us and plants upon us the badge of sonship. In John 1:12 we read, "But as many as received him, to them gave he power to become the sons of God." Yes, it is wonderful to be in Christ. Now let us look at

II. The Promise Given

Here it is, "There is therefore now no condemnation to them which are in Christ Jesus." Here is comfort and encouragement for the Christian. You will sin often, you will not always go God's way, you may have sorrow and trouble in this life, but since you are in Christ, there will never be any condemnation for you. This simply means that God will never bring you up before the Judgment Bar and say, "Now you are going to have to pay for your sins." No, a thousand times no. They are all covered by the blood of

Christ. If you are in Christ, you're a part of Christ. And since He will never be sent to hell, neither will you. Our salvation in Christ is a complete salvation. When a man lays his sin at the foot of the cross and looks by faith into the face of Jesus, he steps out into an experience where there is no condemnation, but gladness, freedom and assurance.

A little girl had been frightened by hearing the preacher talk about the power of Satan. So she asked her father, "Is Satan bigger than I?"

And the father answered, "Yes."

Then she asked, "Is Satan bigger than you?"

And again the father answered, "Yes."

Finally she said, "Is Satan bigger than Jesus Christ?"

"No," answered the father.

"Well then," she said, "I will not care a rap for him."

Yes, Satan is mighty, but he is not almighty. He would like to get hold of us and take us down to the hot pits of hell, but he can't do it. Jesus is greater than Satan. When once you have put your trust in Him, you have won the victory. You will never be condemned.

In the Old Testament days there were six cities of refuge. What was the significance of these cities? Well, suppose two men were working together on a house and one man accidentally killed the other. He would be afraid that the brother of the dead man would seek to kill him, so he would run to the city of refuge. The priests there would receive him and keep him safe until a fair trial could be held. Well, Jesus is our Refuge. You who have sinned can flee to Him, and just as surely as God lives, you will never be condemned.

Christian, how do you feel when you read this text? How do you feel when you remember that you were lost and on the road to hell and Jesus reached down and saved you and gave you a solemn promise that you would never come into condemnation? Oh, you ought to fall down at His feet and thank Him with all of your heart! And then you ought to go out to live more like Him in every way.

Now, I have a word for those who have never trusted Christ as personal Saviour. You are in danger. The sword of judgment hangs over your head. You are already under condemnation. There is just one thing for you to do. Put everything else behind, no matter how precious it is, if that thing keeps you from Christ. Then come to Him in repentance and faith.

A young man went hunting alone in the mountains of New York State. When night came he was lost, many miles from home, weary and hungry. He gathered some pine knots, made a fire and lay down to sleep. When day dawned he awoke, chilled to the bone and very hungry. He wandered aimlessly all day long, then when night came he reached a clearing and thought surely that he would find a cabin there and someone to help him. But to his great dismay, he soon recognized the spot as the same place where he had spent the previous night. He had wandered in a circle and had come back to the starting place. Again he made a fire and spent a miserable night. The next morning he heard a shot. He listened for a few minutes and the shot was repeated. He then raised his own gun and fired into the air. In a short time the searching party found him and he was saved.

That's the picture of many people today. They are lost in the mountains of sin. They have wandered about, thinking of their souls. They have had many noble impulses, many longings to live a better life. But always they come back to the same place of inaction and indecision. But Jesus is seeking you. He came to earth and died to save you. He holds out His loving arms to you today. He wants to save you and give you His best in two worlds.

Why go on without Him? Why will you die? Come to Him and there will never be any condemnation for you.

Sermon 3

THE RICHES OF THE REDEEMED
(PART TWO)

Romans 8:28

The eighth chapter of Romans is one of the greatest chapters in the Bible. If a Christian wants to know how rich he is, just let him bathe his soul in this chapter. In verse 1 we find that there is no condemnation for a Christian. In verse 28 we find that there is no complication for a Christian. In verses 35-39 we find that there is no separation for a Christian. No condemnation — no complication — no separation. You can't beat that trinity of riches for the redeemed!

In our first sermon on this chapter we thought together about "no condemnation." In this message let us think about "no complication" for a Christian. And here it is. "And we know that all things work together for good to them that love God, to them who are the called according to his purpose." In this text, as in verse 1, which says that there is no condemnation to them which are in Christ Jesus, we see the same two great truths standing out, concerning the persons addressed and the promise given.

I. THE PERSONS ADDRESSED

Paul said that he was talking to those who loved God, to those He has called according to His purpose. We see clearly here that God is the primary agent in salvation. He calls us to come to Him. When we respond and are saved, we fall in love with Him. He first loves us, then we love Him. And these are the ones Paul is addressing here. He is not talking to people who do not love God, who trample His Son underfoot, who live in sin. He is talking to those who have been saved, those who love God.

Now the word "purpose" appears here. From all eternity past, God purposed in His heart that He would save all those who came unto Him by faith. Here we find the true meaning of predestination. God did not decree that some people would go to heaven in spite of all their sin, and that some would go to hell in spite of all that they did to be saved. That would be fatalism. That would be condemning a man before he came into the world. But God did foreknow all things. He knew before we were born whether or not we would accept Christ. And He ordained that those who believe in Christ would inherit everlasting life. His foreknowledge came first, then He elected to eternal life all who exercised faith in His Son. This truth is clearly taught in the same eighth chapter of Romans.

What has God promised to the lost? Nothing but an eternal hell. God may allow sinful men in this world to accumulate many things, but they can't take these things with them. So when they come to the end of the way, there is no hope for them. They face hell and all of its fury. They face separation from God and all of His blessings. God holds out no promise of good to those who do not love Him.

So we see that the great promise in this text is given to only one class of people. The promise is to Christians. It is to those whom God has called. It is to those who love God.

II. The Promise Given

"And we know that all things work together for good to them that love God." Paul did not indulge in guesswork when he talked about the things of God. Over and over he said, "I know." He knew because of his close communion with Christ. He knew because of the revelations that he had received from Christ. And he knew because of the personal experience he had had with Christ. We live today in an age of uncertainty. We are uncertain about almost everything. This uncertainty reaches its most dangerous climax in the spiritual realm. There are too many religious leaders who are filled with doubt. They doubt the Word of God. They doubt the virgin birth of Christ. They doubt His miracles. They are not sure that He rose from the grave. They laugh at the idea of His Second Coming.

Now the doubts of these religious leaders have spilled over into the minds of their congregations, causing them to wonder about the truths of God and the reality of religion. But Paul was certain. He was a dogmatist. He never expressed doubt about the great things of God. As you follow him in all that he says and does, you must say, "Here is a man who is sure of himself. Here is a man who knows. Here is a man we can trust."

Now he says here that we know "that all things work together for good." He doesn't say that all things are good. He does say that when God puts them all together, they turn out for our good. Was it a good thing when you met some great disappointment? It didn't seem to be, did it? Was it a good thing when your loved one died and left you broken hearted? It didn't seem so, did it? Was it a good thing when you had that accident and were laid up in the hospital for weeks? It didn't seem to be, did it? Yet one day God works all these things in together and causes you to see that they are all for the best.

You go to the doctor and he gives you a prescription. You take it to the drugstore and the pharmacist begins to fill this prescription. The very first ingredient that he puts in would kill you outright if you took it alone. But he doesn't stop there. He puts in another ingredient and still another. Then when he mixes all these ingredients together you take the medicine and find that it was just what you needed for what ailed you. In like manner, we see that all the things which happen to us in life are not good

The Riches of the Redeemed (Part Two)

things, but when God mixes them all up we see that they work together for our good.

Joseph must have been a happy young man. He was a favorite son of a loving father. He had everything to make life pleasant. Then one day his jealous brothers seized him and mistreated him and finally sold him into slavery. Surely his heart must have been heavy as he was taken down into Egypt. He knew that he wouldn't see his father again. He knew that instead of being a favored son, now he would be nothing but a slave performing menial tasks. Things looked mighty black for him. He had nothing to look forward to. Then the time came when he was thrown into jail because he refused to commit adultery and because he wanted to do right in God's sight. Yonder he is now. He is nothing but a slave, languishing in prison and probably facing death. I go up to the cell door and look through and say, "Cheer up, Joseph, all things work together for good to them that love God."

Then he sadly says to me, "That may be true, but I can't see it now. I am really in trouble. And to make matters worse, I have done nothing wrong."

But several years go by. No longer is he a slave. No longer is he in prison. He is the greatest man in Egypt, his power is next to that of the king. As such he saves a nation and saves his own family and is reunited with his father. I go to the palace to visit him and I say, "Joseph, what about it now?"

He smiles and answers, "Yes, you were right. All things do work together for good to them that love God. I didn't see it then, but I surely do see it now. I thank God that all these tragic things happened to me. God caused them to work out for my good."

Now let's understand what is meant here by the word "good." If we think that all things work together to give us all that we desire, to deliver us from all trouble, to make us all prosperous and to make life one long sweet song, we are going to be badly disappointed. No, all things work together to make us better people and more faithful Christians. The very next verse tells us that these things come to us in order that we might be conformed to the image of Christ.

I see a farmer going out into the orchard to prune his fruit trees. I can imagine the trees saying, "Don't do that. It hurts. Why do you make us suffer this way?" Yet, because of this pruning the trees grow more beautiful and bear more fruit. And that is what will happen to us if we are patient under the chastening hand of God. We will become better children of God in every way. Yet I do want to say that God does reward us, often even materially, because of our faithfulness and patience. Out in California a heavy downpour of rain caused a flood that washed away a mill. The owner grieved over his loss, but after the waters had receded he found a rich vein of gold ore where the mill had been. He never would have found the gold if the mill hadn't been washed away. In a western state a large ranch had one valuable spring which supplied all the water that was needed. One day an earthquake completely ruined this spring. But the next day a bubbling oil well came up in place of the spring.

Oh, in like manner God takes our sorrow, our disappointments, our heartaches, and works them all together for our good and His glory. When God takes something from us, He always gives us something better in its place.

Daniel was one of the finest young men of the Old Testament. The king of Babylon came into Judah, conquered the land, and carried Daniel and certain others into captivity to Babylon. Surely this must have been a sorrow to Daniel's heart. So I say to him, "Daniel, this is pretty rough, isn't it?"

And he replies, "Yes, but I am trusting God. I believe

The Riches of the Redeemed (Part Two)

that some good will come out of this." Then comes a time when he has disobeyed the king's command and they are rushing him off to the lions' den.

Then I say, "Daniel, it's all over now. You don't have a chance. Those lions are hungry and ferocious and they will tear you to pieces in thirty seconds."

But Daniel replies, "I am still trusting God. He will do what is best for me." You know the rest of the story. God sent His angels to shut the mouths of the lions, and he spent a peaceful night. The next day Daniel's enemies were cast into the den of lions and destroyed and Daniel was given the highest honors of the kingdom.

Now I ask Daniel the question, "Do you believe that all things work together for good to them that love God?"

And he says, "Yes, I certainly do. Things may look black for a while, but if you put your faith in God, everything will work out for your good?"

Look at Jesus on the cross. What a black hour it was for Him! He had never sinned, but now He was dying the death of a criminal. He had gone about doing good, but now they were killing Him. But Jesus never flinched. He looked down the ages and saw how His death would be bringing millions home to glory. He rejoiced as He saw all things working together for good.

I believe this: Anything that brings us closer to God is something that is working together for our good. George Matheson was the author of a beautiful song about the love of Christ. This song begins with the words, "Oh, love, that will not let me go." There is a story behind this song. George loved a beautiful girl. They were engaged to be married. Then he developed eye trouble. When he went to a specialist, the doctor said to him, "George, you will be totally blind in a few months." This broke his heart. But he knew where to find comfort. He would go to the girl he loved. Surely she would be a source of strength to him in that hour. But when he told her the sad truth, she said,

"I don't want to be married to a blind man." The engagement was broken and George staggered home with a heavy heart. He sat down in his loneliness and looked out upon a life of shattered dreams and hopes, mourning not only the loss of his eyesight, but the loss of the woman he loved. But in his sorrow, he was drawn closer to God than ever before. It was then that he sang, "Oh, love, that will not let me go." And from that moment forth he became a mightier man for God than ever before. Yes, heartaches often come and troubles overshadow us, but if they serve to bring us closer to God, we know that they are working together for our good.

Now this is one proof that we belong to the Lord. The Bible says, "Whom the Lord loveth, he chasteneth." Chastisement, therefore, is one of the marks to prove that we are the sons of God. Maclaren tells of a man who joined the army while he was just a boy. He was gone from home for many years. When he returned he was so greatly changed that his mother didn't recognize him. But, when he was a little boy, his wrist had been accidentally wounded with a knife. To comfort him, his mother said, "Never mind, son, when you become a man, mother will always know you by the scar on your wrist." But now as a grown man, his mother didn't recognize him. Then the soldier rolled up his sleeve, pointed to the scar, and said, "Mother, don't you recognize that?" Immediately she threw her arms around him. The scar proved that he was her son.

And we, too, can know that we are the children of God because He corrects and disciplines us. But all of it is in love and all of it works together for our good.

You go into a factory where they weave cloth and you walk down one side of the looms. You see that most of the threads are white, but here and there you find a dark thread. You wonder why the dark thread is there. Why aren't all the threads white? But then you go around to the other side of the looms and you understand. You realize that the dark threads were put in to weave beautiful flowers into the cloth. And as Christians stand on this side of God's great loom of life and see the things that go into the making of character, they notice that God often puts the dark threads among the white. Why aren't all the threads white? Why aren't all of our days bright? Why do we have so many unhappy experiences mingled with the pleasant things of life? We don't know now, but someday when we stand on the other side of life's loom, we will see that God used the dark threads to make life more beautiful and useful for us all.

Then surely we will say with Paul, "I know now that all things work together for good to them that love God."

Sermon 4

THE RICHES OF THE REDEEMED
(PART THREE)

Romans 8:35-39

Again we are counting up the "riches of the redeemed" as we find them in Romans 8. In our first message on this chapter we learned that there is "no condemnation" for them that are in Christ Jesus. In our second message we saw that for the Christian there is "no complication," since all things work together for his good. Now we come to the climax of this great chapter and find that there is "no separation" from God for one of His children. What a rich storehouse of grace is here for believers. They will never be condemned, everything will work out for their good, and they will never be separated from God and His love. Selah! Selah! Think of that!

I. PAUL ASKS AN IMPORTANT QUESTION

We hear him saying, "Who shall separate us from the love of Christ?" Now what is bound up in that love? No one can fully answer that question. All that we know is that we were sinners, on the way to hell, and that He loved us enough to leave the glories of heaven and come to earth to suffer and die in our stead, that we might live forever with Him. Neither can anyone fully describe all the agony and heartbreak wrapped up in His leaving heaven, His humiliation on earth, and his death on Calvary.

We just know that Christ loved us poor sinners more than any man ever loved his wife, more than any mother ever loved her child, more than any patriot ever loved his

The Riches of the Redeemed (Part Three)

country. He loved not just in words, but in deeds. He said on one occasion, "Greater love hath no man than this, that a man lay down his life for his friends." And He not only said it — He did it. He laid down His life for those who had sinned against Him, and broken His laws. He laid down His life even for those who put Him to death. Most people have someone they are not particularly fond of. Would you go out today and lay down your life for that one? I am afraid not. But no one ever mistreated you as they did Jesus, yet the great love in His heart drove Him to die even for those who hated Him most.

In the early days of our country a prairie fire swept through the middle west. A rescue party went out to help and came upon a burned cottage. On the ground they saw a black object. One of them went over to this object and found that it was a dead hen. Her body was burned almost to a cinder, but her wings were spread wide. He kicked the dead hen and three little chickens ran out from under her. The hen had sat still in the midst of the flames, covering her chickens. She gave her own life that her little chickens might live. That's what Jesus did. He gave His own life that we might be saved. He went to the cross to save us from eternal death. Oh, the length and the breadth and the width and the height of Christ's love! Who can separate us from such love? Paul answers the question in some of the most stirring and uplifting words in the Bible.

II. Paul Says That the Seven Tragic Experiences of Life Cannot Separate Us from Christ's Love

Now three of these are inward experiences while the other four are outward experiences. The inward experiences are tribulation, distress and persecution. They may originate from outside sources, but the heartbreak and the suffering are on the inside. Every one of us has had these minutes of anguish. No one was beating us, no one was causing us physical agony, but deep down inside we carried heavy hearts. We could not sleep at night and we had no peace by day. Nothing in the world, however pleasant or beautiful or interesting, could long divert our minds from this soul-suffering. And what was the thing which finally gave us peace? It was the smile of God upon us. It was something He did for us in His mighty love. We came to learn that His face was shining behind the clouds and soon life was brighter and better again.

Dr. R. G. Lee tells of going hunting in the woods with his little boy. The sun seemed to drop out of sight, clouds arose, the wind began to blow and the night-birds began to cry out. The little boy was frightened and said, "Dad, have you been here before?"

"Yes," answered his father.

"And do you know the way out so that we can get home?" the little boy asked.

"Yes, son, I know the way out," the father replied. Then the boy gave a big sigh of relief. Oh, we are often in the dark forests of trouble, but Jesus says, "I know the way out. Just put your hand in Mine and I will bring you safely through."

A man tells about sailing across the Pacific many years ago. The trip took eleven days but for ten days they ploughed through a furious storm that shook the boat. It was so dark that they could hardly see their way. The passengers were anxious and scared. But one voice calmed their fears and everyone came to listen for that voice. It was the voice of the man in the crow's nest. Every hour he would cry out the time and say, "All's well!! All's well!" And as we are shaken by these inner storms, if we will but listen, we can hear the voice of Jesus saying, "All is well. I am still on the throne. I love you and am watching over you. I will never leave you nor forsake you. I will bring you through all of these difficulties."

The four outward experiences listed here are famine, nakedness, peril and sword. We in America know little

The Riches of the Redeemed (Part Three)

about these things. We have plenty to eat, good clothes to wear, and so far the wars of earth have not ravaged our land. But if these things do come, we can remember that Christ is still present and these things can't destroy Him, neither can they separate us from His love.

As a great Scotch Christian lay dying, he asked his daughter to place his finger on the eighth chapter of Romans. Then with a smile on his face he said, "My children, I had breakfast with you this morning, but I am going to have supper tonight with the Lord Jesus." The scientists tell us that there are such destructive forces in the world today that all of our great cities and all that is in them could be wiped out in a matter of seconds. Does this scare you? It should not if you are a Christian. It just means breakfast here and supper with the Lord Jesus in heaven. The most destructive bombs in the world can't separate us from the love of Christ.

Paul goes on to say here that we are more than conquerors through Him that loved us. When Lord Nelson reported to the British Admiralty his great victory over the French fleet in the battle of the Nile, he said that the word "victory" was not large enough to use in describing what took place. And when Paul speaks of the victories the Christian wins over all the forces that fight against him, the great word "conqueror" is not enough. He says we are more than conquerors through Him that loved us.

Perhaps Paul had witnessed one of the triumphant processions of a Roman conqueror. The Roman general would fare forth to other lands to fight for Rome. Then, having vanquished the enemy, he would return to Rome. A great parade would be held, witnessed by the emperor and thousands of Roman citizens. The general would ride at the head of his victorious legions, arrayed in silken garments and crowned with garlands. Behind his chariot, with chains about their necks, would walk the princes and kings he had taken captive. And after him would come other chariots and floats, depicting the victorious incidents of the battle. Behind these would come all the brave soldiers who had fought with the conqueror. Indeed, this was a high day in Rome. Now Paul had witnessed this picture of victory and glory. He had looked upon the conqueror, but thinking of the Great Conqueror, Jesus Christ, and of the victories won through Him, he exclaimed, "We are more than conquerors!"

Oh, if we will stay close to Christ and lean on Him and receive His grace, we, too, shall be more than conquerors. Then other people will see how we have come through and they will say, "He couldn't have done that by himself. He couldn't have borne that burden if he had not had another One to help him." And in our hearts we will know that it was Christ who gave us the victory.

III. Paul Says That Our Ten Strong Opponents Cannot Separate Us from the Love of Christ

Here is the list, "I am persuaded that neither death, nor life, nor angels, nor principalities, nor powers, nor things present, nor things to come, nor height, nor depth, nor any other creature shall be able to separate us from the love of God which is in Christ Jesus our Lord." Did you ever hear such an array of those things which could harm us? But Paul says that none nor all of these things can separate us from the Divine Love.

Surely this is a great proof text for eternal security. Some people feel that if they commit one sin after they are saved, they will be lost. If that were true, there would be no hope for any of us. But if none of these seven experiences and ten opponents can separate us from the love of God, surely one or two little sins won't do it. Of course, this truth doesn't give a Christian a license to go out and sin. If you continually follow sin, it proves that you are not a Christian. A real Christian may fall, but he doesn't continue in sin. The difference is seen in Peter and Judas. Judas sinned,

The Riches of the Redeemed (Part Three)

but he never repented of his sin. He never was saved. He was a devil all the time. Jesus said so. But Peter was brokenhearted after his sin. He wept bitterly and repented and came back to live a great life for Christ.

We are told here that life and all of its problems and death and all of its terrors cannot separate us from the love of God. We are told that God's angels can't separate us, neither can any authority or power on earth. We are told that the things which now exist and the things which are coming in the future cannot separate us. We are told that neither height nor depth nor anything which God created can separate us from His love. When Oliver Cromwell lay dying he said, "I think I am the poorest wretch that lives, but I am loved of God."

Niagara Falls pours millions of gallons of water every hour upon the rocks below. As you look at the falls you think that no power on earth could stop this flow of water. But there have been times when the flow ceased. Sometimes in the winter ice dams up the river, the waters fail and the great musical roar is hushed. But there never will be a time when God's love fails.

Here is the greatest thought that can ever possess the mind of a believer. God is love and we are right in the middle of that love through our faith in the Lord Jesus Christ. Isn't it wonderful to know that God loves you and will never let anything come between you and that love. A scoffing infidel argued religion with a fine Christian woman. She was unable to answer all of his questions. Finally he said to her, "You don't know what you believe."

"But," she replied, "I know whom I have believed."

You and I may not have all the answers, we may not be able to meet all the theological difficulties presented to us, but by faith we can know Jesus Christ and when we know Him peace comes in our hearts and we can leave all of our questions up to Him.

A certain retail merchant has an impressive trade mark.

It is in the form of a circle across which his name is written. Underneath are the words, "I never disappoint." That's Jesus. He never disappoints in life, He never disappoints in death, He never disappoints in heaven. And nothing can separate us from Him and His love.

A little boy was told by his father to wait on a certain corner while he had an automobile tire changed. The car required more work than the father expected and he was gone from his son for over an hour. He hurried back to find his little boy right where he had told him to stay. He said to him, "Did you think daddy had forgotten you?"

And the little boy replied, "Oh, no, I knew you would come as soon as you could. I wasn't a bit worried. I stayed where you told me to stay and I waited and watched for you."

Oh, dear Christian, worried and confused by life's problems, you should be just like that little boy! Just remember that Christ loves you and in perfect trust wait and watch for His coming in perfect obedience, remembering always that nothing in the world can separate you from the love of God which is in Christ Jesus our Lord.

Sermon 5

THE SWEETEST NAME I KNOW

Philippians 2:5-11

Many years ago Shakespeare asked the question, "What's in a name?" He said that a rose by any other name would smell just as sweet. In a sense that is true. You could call a rose a stinkweed or a skunk blossom and not change the fragrance of that rose. But in another sense a name means everything. If I were to give you my check for $10,000, they would laugh at you at the bank and tell you that the check was not worth it. But if you could get a check from Henry Ford or Nelson Rockefeller for a million dollars, you could laugh and say, "I am a rich man." It's the name that makes the difference — there is something in a name.

If I announced that I was going to preach at the Coliseum tomorrow night, a few of our faithful members would be there. If I announced that Billy Graham was going to preach out there, the place would be packed. Names do mean something. So I come to talk to you about the Name that is above every Name — the Name of Jesus. Ah, there is a name that means something! It means something in heaven — it means something on earth — it even means something in hell.

> Jesus is the sweetest name I know,
> And He's just the same as His lovely name,
> And that's the reason why I love Him so,
> For Jesus is the sweetest name I know.

There are five things that I would like to say about the Name of Jesus: It is a powerful Name, it is a sacrificial Name, it is a conquering Name, it is an exalted Name, it is a saving Name.

I. THE NAME OF JESUS IS A POWERFUL NAME

Just think of the names in the past which denoted power. Alexander the Great had a powerful name. At the age of thirty-three he had conquered the known world, but at thirty-three he died in drunkenness and debauchery and his name lost its power. Caesar had a powerful name. He led the Roman legions to conquer one land after another. But one day a dagger in the hand of his friend, Brutus, conquered him. His name lost its power. Napoleon had a powerful name. He brought Europe to her knees before him. But he met his Waterloo and died in exile on the island of St. Helena. His name lost its power. The Kaiser and Hitler and Mussolini had powerful names. They frightened the world. Every one of them went down into inglorious defeat. Their names lost their power.

But not so with Jesus. He had power to create the world. He has power to change the course of history and the destiny of nations. He had power over death and disease. He had power over death and the grave. His power has never diminished and some day all of heaven and hell and earth will come to feel that power.

France once boasted of the power of Louis the Great. It was said that he was the one great man of the world. But one day he was conquered by death. At his funeral the great cathedral was packed by mourners, prominent people from all walks of life. They came to pay a final tribute to the one whom they considered great. The cathedral was dark except for one lone candle which shone over the golden casket. At the appointed hour Massilon, the court preacher, stood up to address the assembly. He slowly reached over and snuffed out the one candle which had been put there to symbolize the greatness of the king. Then from the darkness came just four words, "God only is great." How true that is. Men of this world claim greatness and power for a while, then death cuts them off. Only the Almighty Christ retains His power throughout all the ages.

Today we look out upon a world where it seems that Satan has the upper hand. In government, in politics, in business, in sports, in society, in recreation we see the hand of the evil one. This is his day. Satan is the prince of the world. He is running things. But this won't always be true. One day Jesus is going to come back and take over. Then every knee shall bow and every tongue shall confess that He is Lord to the glory of God the Father.

II. THE NAME OF JESUS IS A SACRIFICIAL NAME

He sacrificed all the joys and glories of heaven for you and me. He held the highest position in glory. He was the central figure in heaven. The angels and the archangels ran to do His bidding. The saints in glory sang His praises, crying out, "Holy, Holy, Holy, Lord God of hosts!" But for our sakes He gave up all of that. He shed the garments of glory, turned His back upon all that was dearest to Himself and came down to earth to suffer and die as our Saviour. "He humbled Himself and became obedient unto death, even the death of the cross" for our sakes.

Suppose that Queen Elizabeth were to denounce her throne and go down into the slums of London to become a scrub woman for the poorest family there for the rest of her life. Her condescension would not compare with the step downward which Jesus took when He left heaven's glory for earth's gloom. In heaven all things were His. Here He had no home that He could call His own, He had no bed where He might lay His head. He had no table where He might enjoy a meal. He had to live upon the bounty of others. The richest of the rich in heaven became the poorest of the poor on earth. The highest of the high in heaven became the lowest of the low on earth. The greatest of the great in heaven became a servant on earth for our sakes.

How could He love me so?
How could He love me so?
How could my Saviour to Calvary go?
How could He love me so?

There is an old legend which tells us how Jesus became our Saviour. God called all of the hosts of heaven before Him. He described to them the lost condition of mankind and told them what one must be and do in order to come down to the earth to save lost humanity. The first requirement was that the Saviour must be without sin. Various ones in heaven came before God and offered to come to earth and redeem mankind.

Abraham, the friend of God, the father of the faithful, came first and said, "I will go, Father. Let me go down and give myself for the redemption of the lost."

But God had to say, "No, Abraham, you do not measure up. There was sin in your life when you lived upon the earth."

Then Moses came. He was the great leader of Israel, the greatest man in the Old Testament. He said, "Let me go, Father. Let me go and shed my blood for the sins of the earth."

But God had to say, "No, Moses, I brought you home to heaven, but your sin on earth kept you out of the Promised Land. You cannot go."

Then David, the sweet singer of Israel, the man after God's own heart, came forward. "Let me go, Father," he said. "Let me give my life for lost sinners."

But God had to say, "No, David, you sinned grievously and you cannot go."

Then Jesus came before the throne and said, "Father, I love lost sinners. Let Me go and give My life for their redemption." The legend then tells us that all of heaven broke out with protests and outbursts of opposition.

"No! No!" they cried. "The Only-begotten Son must not go and give Himself away for sinful men."

But Jesus looked into the Father's face and said, "Yes,

Father. I must go. Greater love hath no man than this, that he give his life for his friends." God then gave His consent. Jesus sped past the moon and the stars and the sun and came to earth to live and die for us. Oh, what condescension!

Now sacrifice means suffering. Did anyone ever suffer like Jesus? When Judas planted the kiss of betrayal upon his cheek, He suffered. When vile men spat their foul saliva into His face, He suffered. When rough men slapped Him over and over again, He suffered. When the steel of the scourge cut deep gashes in His back, He suffered. When they pressed the crown of thorns down upon His brow, He suffered. When they nailed His hands and feet to the cross, He suffered. When they lifted the cross and it fell into the hole prepared for it, He suffered, and when the nails tore through His flesh, He suffered. When His lips became parched and His mouth hot as an oven, He suffered. When He cried, "My God, my God, why hast thou forsaken me?" He suffered most of all. When He cried, "It is finished," and gave up the ghost, He suffered. Yes, no one ever suffered like Jesus and it was all for you and me. No one ever cared for us like He did.

III. THE NAME OF JESUS IS A CONQUERING NAME

Jesus always conquers. He never lost a battle. When Satan came against Him with three fierce temptations, Jesus beat him back every time. When men sought to defeat Him in debate, He overcame them every time. And even when He died upon the cross, although it seemed that He was meeting defeat, He was finishing a salvation which would conquer millions of hearts and finally put Satan into the Lake of Fire. The text tells us that His is a conquering name on earth. There are many men who will not bow to Him now, but the day is coming when every knee will bow and every tongue shall confess that He is Lord. The text tells us that His is a conquering name in hell. The time will come when all those who have rejected

Him will be down in hell and they will cringe every time they hear the name of Jesus.

Now the conqueror always controls, so I would like to ask you a personal question. You have permitted Christ to come into your heart. Do you let Him control your life? Does He have first place with you? Or do you live for your own convenience and comfort?

One day God had a big job for Moses. He said to Moses, "What is that in your hand?"

And Moses replied, "It is a rod." He was probably surprised that God would even notice such a small thing as this stick, but God was teaching him a great lesson.

"Lay it down," commanded the Lord. Well, Moses put the stick down on the ground and immediately it turned into a hissing, writhing serpent.

Now God says, "Pick it up again." That was not so easy — no one likes to pick up a snake. But Moses picked up the snake and it became a stick again. And under God, Moses used that stick to do mighty things for the Lord. Maybe God wants you to serve Him in a better way. He says, "Lay down that habit which is hindering you. Lay down that hot temper. Lay down that critical spirit. Lay down that secret sin. Lay down that indifference and neglectful attitude." And then God would have you to take up what is left of your life and use it to serve Him.

Oh, may the Spirit of God work so mightily upon us that we will want to tear our hearts wide open before the Lord, throw out everything that is wrong there, and fill those hearts with His plans and purposes.

God tells the Christian that He will "preserve" him. Do you know what it means when a woman preserves fruit? Let us say that she wants to preserve some peaches. She cuts up the peaches, puts them in a vessel, adds sugar, then lets them simmer over a slow fire until they come to a boil. Then she stirs them up some more, adds more sugar and lets them boil until they are preserved. What has she done?

She has fixed those peaches so that they will keep and so they will keep sweet. In like manner God puts the Christian through many processes. He not only wants to keep us but He wants to keep us sweet for His service. That's the difference between preserves and pickles. Pickles will keep just as well as preserves, but they will keep sour.

So here is the lesson — let Jesus, the Conqueror, control you. Surrender to Him as Lord and Master and let Him keep you sweet and useful as a Christian.

IV. THE NAME OF JESUS IS AN EXALTED NAME

We read that "God hath highly exalted him and given him a name that is above every name." Mary did not give Him this name. Joseph didn't give Him this name. An angel didn't give Him this name. God gave Him this name. No one but God had an adequate conception of the mighty things that Christ would do down through the ages, so no one but God was capable of bestowing upon Him the name that is above every name.

Richard Whitney had a good name. His ancestors came over from England. His father was president of a Boston bank. His brother was a partner in J. P. Morgan Company. Richard was a leader in prep school and college. He married the daughter of an eminent family. He bought a seat on the New York Stock Exchange for $65,000. Five times he was elected president of the Exchange. He signed two thousand membership certificates for the Exchange members. Then one day they found that he had misappropriated funds which had been entrusted to him. He lost his good name, he lost his big job, he was sent to prison for five years. Then the New York Stock Exchange called in all the certificates which he had signed, erased his name, and had them signed by the new president. The name of Richard Whitney was no longer a good name for a broker to have hanging on his wall. But Jesus' Name is just the opposite. Down here His name had shame and disgrace heaped upon it — now God has exalted that name above all the names of heaven and earth.

If the throne of heaven were vacant and if I were given an opportunity to choose one worthy to sit upon that throne, I might think of many men of the earth who bore illustrious names. I would think of the Apostle Paul, the mightiest man of God who ever walked the earth. I would think of all of his great accomplishments, I would think of his love for Christ, I would think of his death for Christ's sake. But I would be forced to say, "Paul, as great as you are, the throne of heaven is beyond you." Then I would think of George Washington, the father of our country. He was a great warrior, a great statesman, a noble character. But I would be forced to say to him, "George Washington, you were a great man, but pass on, the throne is for One higher than you." Then I would think of Spurgeon, the mighty preacher. He preached to thousands of people and won thousands of them to Christ. He wrote many books which are still influencing the world, but I would be forced to say to Spurgeon, "Pass on, great preacher, the throne is for One higher than you." Then I would think of D. L. Moody. He had very little education, but he used it all for the glory of God. He broke the King's English, but he also broke hearts for Christ. And when he died he carried many souls to glory with him. But I would be forced to say, "Pass on, great and good man of God, the throne is for One higher than you."

Then I see Jesus. His head is crowned with a crown of thorns. His hands and feet bear the marks of the nails. His face is covered with blood and spittle. As I look upon these things, I know that He bore them all for me and I say, "Thou art worthy. Thou hast loved us with an everlasting love. Thou hast given Thy life for our redemption. Mount the throne, O Blessed One, for it is Thine! Bring forth the royal diadem and crown Him Lord of all." And as He takes His place upon the throne I behold a great transformation.

Instead of the crown of thorns He wears a crown of heavenly jewels. Instead of the garments of a peasant, He wears the purple robes of glory. Instead of a blood-stained face, I see a face of shining beauty and glory. And I hear heaven's hosts ring out with the song,

> Worthy is the Lamb that was slain to receive
> Power and riches and wisdom and strength and
> Honor and glory and blessing.

Yes, the name of Jesus is and shall be an exalted name.

V. The Name of Jesus Is a Saving Name

"Thou shalt call His name Jesus, for he shall save his people from their sins." "As many as received him, to them gave he the power to become the sons of God." "There is none other name under heaven, given among men, whereby we must be saved," except the name of Jesus. "Whosoever calleth upon the name of the Lord shall be saved."

Call upon your goodness and there is no salvation there. Call upon your good works and there is no salvation there. Call upon your charitable gifts, and there is no salvation there. Call upon your religious formalities and there is no salvation there. But call upon Jesus and you will find full salvation.

As a poor motherless boy, I had a great longing in my heart for something that would bring me happiness and peace and companionship. Because of our poverty I was denied the privileges given to other boys. We lived on the wrong side of the tracks. I went to a revival meeting as a barefoot lonely boy. I heard the gospel songs and the gospel sermon. I saw others go down the aisle and give themselves to Jesus. I left the meeting each night with tears in my eyes and heaviness of guilt upon my heart. I walked past the cemetery where my mother was buried, went home and wept myself to sleep. I wanted to be a Christian, but I felt that I was too poor to belong to a church and no one took an interest in my soul. But my tears didn't save me. My desires didn't save me. Years later on a Sunday afternoon after Billy Sunday had preached, I walked down the aisle and the best I knew how I trusted Christ as my Saviour.

Years have gone by since that time. God has blessed me in a million ways and the people have honored me and I have a hope in my heart that nothing can take away. And it all started when I looked into the face of Jesus that day and claimed Him as my Saviour. Thank God, He saves and keeps.

A sailor boy who was shipwrecked clung to a plank and was washed ashore. He was taken to a hospital. The chaplain came to see him and tried to win him to Christ. The boy didn't seem to understand the way of salvation, so the chaplain asked him, "What did you do when you were thrown into the sea?"

And the boy answered, "I caught hold of the plank, rested upon it and it brought me to shore."

"That's it," said the chaplain, "Jesus Christ is the plank. He wants you to rest upon Him for eternal salvation. If you do that He will bear you safely through life's voyage and into the harbor of heaven at the end of the way."

Twenty years later the chaplain was in another hospital. They asked him to speak to a sailor who was dying. When he went over to the man's bed, the man recognized him and said, "The plank bears, sir. The plank bears."

And the chaplain said, "What do you mean?"

The man answered, "Do you remember twenty years ago speaking to a sailor who had been shipwrecked and urging him to rest his hope upon Christ even as he had rested his body upon the plank in the ocean? Well, sir, for twenty years I have rested upon that plank. Christ has carried me safely through the storms of life and now He is going to take me into the heavenly harbor at last."

Yes, Jesus' Name is a saving name. He will never let you down if you trust Him. If you have never trusted Him, won't you do it now? He is Almighty to save. He is just waiting to receive you.

Sermon 6

MY GOD AND I

Matthew 6:33

Man is one of the weakest animals on earth. The lion, the tiger, the bear, the elephant are all far stronger than he is. Yet man has the greatest work to do on the earth. God put him here and told him to subdue the earth, and to plan and carry out the work of the world. The world would be just one big jungle without man. But how can a weak man do all that is required of him? Certainly not by himself. He needs a partner. And God comes and says, "I will be that partner. I have unlimited power. Link your life with mine and together we will do great things." He says that to men of science, to men of research, to men of medicine, to men of education, to men in all walks of life. And as they have done that they have used God's resources and developed everything from a safety pin to a rocket that reaches the moon. But man by himself could do none of these things — it has been man plus God.

But above all other callings of life, God says to the Christian, "Without Me you can do nothing. Come unto Me — link your life with Mine, then the great spiritual tasks of the world will be accomplished, My name will be glorified and you will be blessed and rewarded." My text for this sermon is my favorite text for the conduct of a Christian. It contains a mighty command and a marvelous promise. "Seek ye first the kingdom of God and his righteousness." That is our part. "All these things shall be added unto you." That is God's part. So you can see that you are to be God's partner. You are to put His interests first always and everywhere. Then God out of His bountiful storehouse will give you everything that you need. Friends, the beautiful thing about it is that it works. And why shouldn't it work? Here are two people walking down the road. One is rich, powerful and good. He loves the other man, although the other man is poor and weak and sinful. Surely, if the poor man strives to please the other man, the other man will provide his every need. Well, God and you are walking the highway which leads to heaven. You are poor and needy, but God has everything. Above all, He loves you. He tells you to walk in His way and then He will give you all that you need. He keeps His promise. It works. Put God and His interests first and He will supply your every need.

I. How You Can Put God and His Interests First

Let us remember now that this text is for the children of God. And like a loving father, God says, "Children, do thus and so and I will reward you." Now there is just one way to become a child of God. You must come to Him by faith in His Son, the Lord Jesus Christ. "As many as received Him, to them gave He the power to become the sons of God." After you have been born again, after you have been born into the family of God, He says unto you, "You are My child now. You are a partner in My business. Put My interests first, and I will give you all that you need." It is wonderful that a great God proposes a bargain like that to a little man on earth, one among millions. But that is just like God. Now how can we put Him first?

A. *We can put Him first in our living.* I rode along one day with a man who said to me, "It is not easy to live as a Christian should. I am tempted every day."

I said to him, "You must keep your Christian profession before you all the time. Not one minute must you forget that you are a child of God. Wherever you are, you must remember that you are a Christian and that there are certain things that you cannot do." And that's it — in order to be a real Christian you must keep a constant watch over self.

Christian living has two sides, the positive and the negative. There are some things you can't do. There are some places you can't go. But just putting these things out of your life doesn't make you a strong Christian. You are not only to be good, you are to be good for something. You are not only to be good, you are to do good. Christian separation has two aspects. It is a separation from the bad things, and a separation unto the good things. So if you are going to put God first, you must take a definite stand. You must say, "There are some things that I am going to do, and some things that I am not going to do." Then having taken a stand, you must stick to it.

There is nothing in the world that has more influence than a consecrated Christian life. Several years ago I was teaching from the Book of Acts in one of our summer assemblies. One morning we studied about the conversion of Saul, who became Paul, the mighty Apostle. After the class a man came up to me and said, "I was saved four years ago. I was like Paul. I was the chief of sinners. But now for four years I have been trying to live for the Lord." I am always interested in causes, so I asked him what was the greatest influence in his conversion. Unhesitatingly he replied, "It was the life of my consecrated wife. For twenty-seven years she not only prayed for me; but she lived such a wonderful Christian life before me that I was caused to see my need of Christ."

Billy Sunday once addressed a letter simply, "God's Man, Adrian, Michigan." The postmaster in that town was not bewildered. He handed the letter over to the man whom he knew to be living closest to God. It was the right man. Can anyone look into your life and say, "He is God's man. She is God's woman. He reminds me of Jesus. She reminds me of Jesus"? The Christians of the New Testament were so different from the others and so separated from sin that people took note of them, that they had been with Jesus. How is your life counting? Does anyone ever say of you, "He is different. He has met Jesus, and there has been a change in his life"?

Sometime ago in Pennsylvania one hundred birds were found dead at the foot of the statue of William Penn. What caused their death? They were migrating south and in the darkness they struck the statue. They were simply flying too low. That's the tragedy of so many lives today. Christians are living on the low level. They are giving their lives to worldly things when they ought to be putting God first in every area of life. The end of a worldly life is spiritual calamity. Oh, if you love God, you ought to put Him first in your living.

B. *We can put Him first in our loyalties.* Our first loyalty is to Christ, His Son. No other person, no other pleasure, no other thing in the world should come before Him. When He saw us on the road to hell, He put us first. He didn't think of His own pleasure or comfort, He was thinking of us. This cost Him His life, but He was loyal to us. Life is filled with choices. As we consider these choices, we need to remember our loyalty to Christ. We ought to say, "He is first in my life. In view of that fact, which choice must I make?" If you do that you will choose always the highest and the best. Are you being loyal to Christ? When you go to the places He does not approve of, when you do the things which do not please Him, when you say the things that you ought not to say, when you spend your money in the wrong way?

Jesus loved everyone. He loved even the sinners who rebelled against Him. He loved even those who put Him to death. Then He told us that we are to love others in the same way, regardless of who they are or what they do to us. Are you being loyal to Him when your heart is black with hatred? Is that the Christlike spirit? You may preach from the pulpit, you may sing in the choir, you may teach a class, you may lead a group, but if your own heart is filled with the wrong spirit, how much good are you going to do? If we are loyal to Christ, we will have something of His spirit in us. Then we cannot keep the wrong spirit in our hearts. We will love everyone, regardless. Yes, I wish that all of us were loyal to Christ under all circumstances. We should ask the question, "What would He do under these same circumstances?" Then we should try to follow in His footsteps.

Then we ought to be loyal to His church. Here is a rich man, whose greatest interest is in an orphans' home. He gives his money and time and efforts to this home. As he lies upon his deathbed, he calls his best friend to his side and says to him, "I am leaving millions of dollars to you. I want you to use most of it for your own benefit, but I want you to use a small part for the orphans' home. I love that home, it is the closest thing on earth to my heart. I want you to take care of it." What should be the duty of that friend? Surely, it would be his duty to look after the interests of this one who has given him so much. It would be criminal if he didn't do that. Well, one day Jesus died on a cross. He left everything good to you and me. But He said, "I love my church. I want you as my child to belong to it. I want you to give it your best. I want you to take care of the thing which is dearest to my heart."

Are you loyal to His church? Some people drop in to the church just once in a while. Is that loyalty? Some give a dollar after they have indulged themselves in everything else. Is that loyalty? Some never serve the church. Is that loyalty? Some never invite anyone else to the church. Is that loyalty? Man has built many institutions. Christ built only one — His church. You are loyal to your club, your lodge, your political party, your school. I tell you that you ought to be loyal to the church, Christ's institution. Your work in these other things and your gifts to them will die with the setting sun. What you do for Christ and His church abides forever.

The best satisfactions of life are found in His church.

A ship was sailing from the Orient, with several cages of birds on board. Far out at sea, one of these birds escaped. In an ecstasy of delight this bird swept through the air. It was free. But in a few hours the poor bird fell back upon the deck of the ship, breathless, struggling, exhausted. He had found no place on the boundless deep to plant his feet. He was glad to come back home. If you are a real Christian, you may leave the church and go out into the world, seeking delight for your soul in earthly things. But you will find no satisfaction until you come back home to the church.

I am thinking now of a certain woman in my home city. She was active in every department of the church life. Then she had some slight difference with the pastor, left the church and sought her happiness in the world. The last time I saw her, she said, "I have gone back to the church. I could not find any happiness or satisfaction outside of the church." Neither can you, if you are a Christian. So I say that you ought to be loyal to His church.

C. *We can put Him first in our loving.* Now if we love Him, we will talk to Him. And God has provided a way for us to do this through the exercise called prayer. God is not far off — He is not behind the veil. He is "closer than hands and feet and nearer than breathing." You and I can go straight to His heart through the Lord Jesus Christ. If someone offered you a million dollars never to pray again, you would be making a bad bargain if you closed that deal. If the twelve apostles lived next door to you, and you had the opportunity to talk to them every day, it would be an injury to your soul if this conversation drew you away from the place of prayer.

Charles F. Kettering was the chief engineer of General Motors. In his time he was the greatest man in America in the field of mechanics. At a banquet a man watched Mr. Kettering's big strong hands, then he asked him the question, "Mr. Kettering, what is the most important thing you ever did with these hands?"

And Mr. Kettering replied, humbly, "The most important thing I ever did with these hands was to fold them in prayer to my Heavenly Father." Yes, if you love Christ and want to put Him first, you will pray.

Then if you love Christ, you will listen to Him. When your loved ones are far away and you call them by long distance, you love to hear their voices. Now you can hear God's voice as you read the Bible. The average Christian hears the Word of God only on Sunday morning as the pastor reads the Scripture. This is not enough. You ought to read the Bible for yourself and remember that God is talking to you.

Then if you love Christ, you will show it by your giving. You tell me that you love your wife with all of your heart, but then I see her wearing shabby clothes and I learn that you do not even provide enough for her to eat. Then I know that you don't love her. We are to love in deeds, not simply in words. Sometime ago I saw a double cartoon. One side of the cartoon showed a man buying ten-dollar tickets to a show. He said to the ticket agent, "Give me the best in the house." In the other picture, he was sitting in the church. A songbook was in his hand and he was singing, "Oh, how I love Jesus." At the same time he was dropping a nickel in the offering plate.

God's Word is specific about the matter of giving. It tells us how much we are to give. The tithe is to be the minimum and we can get a great joy out of going beyond that. It tells us where to bring the tithe. We are to bring it to God's storehouse. This can mean nothing but the church. It tells what the tithe is to be used for. It is to be used for God's work, to glorify Him and to win souls. It tells us then what He will do. He says that He will open up the windows of heaven and pour out a blessing upon us. The blessings do flow when we tithe.

You believe that God created the world, don't you? You believe that Christ died for our sins, don't you? You believe in the judgment, heaven and hell, don't you? Yes, you believe in these things because they are taught in the Bible. Well, the Bible says more about giving than it does about these other matters. Because of its teachings, you ought to pay the tithe. Which do you love most, the Almighty God or the almighty dollar? That's the wrong name for a dollar, anyway. The dollar is not almighty — it does not bring happiness nor contentment, it does not build character, it can never take you home to heaven.

A great giver was once asked how he could give so much. He said, "I shovel out and God shovels in and God uses a bigger shovel than mine." Yes, God says that if we give He will also give to us, heaped up, pressed down, running over.

But someone says, "I can't afford to tithe." You can't afford not to. You will miss too many blessings. I can tell you from personal experience that God blesses the tither in a million ways. But someone says, "I am in debt." You are the very one who ought to tithe. God will help you to pay those debts. When I came out of school I owed $2,200. That was certainly a big debt in those days. But I remembered God's promise and kept on tithing. He brought me out of debt quicker than it could have happened otherwise. Then someone says, "I have a family to care for." You are the very one who ought to tithe. Let God help you with that family. Then someone says, "I am starting a new business." Well, you ought to tithe because you need God as your partner. Then someone says, "I have just enough now." You are the very one who ought to tithe, because then God will make the other nine-tenths go farther.

God has a double purpose in commanding you to tithe. First, He wants others to know of His Son, how He died for them, and how He can save them from sin. If all Christians would tithe, God's work would move forward on the wings of glory.

One day a missionary in Africa went with his party to a village where the natives had never seen a white man. The villagers surrounded them and they feared that bodily harm would be done to them. Instead the chief walked over and took hold of the missionary's hand and said, "Where is the river in which you washed your hands so clean?" Oh, let me tell you something, men's hearts are black with sin. They are lost. Where can they find the fountain that cleanses, the blood that saves? You and I know. It's Jesus, Blessed Jesus. But it's not enough for us to know. We must give so that others can know.

God's other purpose in telling you to tithe is to develop you as a Christian. How much of a Christian do you want to be? Are you content just to go to heaven? If you have trusted Christ as your Saviour, you are on the way to heaven, but is that enough? You can't be the best Christian, the most effective Christian, unless you say, "Lord, I'll go your way."

It's a fine thing to be able to have money if you don't make it your god, if you use it to glorify your Heavenly Father. But it is tragic to let money grip your soul and take you to hell. That which you give to God lifts you heavenward. That which you grasp takes you down to hell. Once I knew a man who was a millionaire, but he was not a Christian. His wife said about him, "His money is taking him down to hell." But God wants us to give so as to free us from the chains of greed and covetousness. A wealthy man who had given thousands of dollars to his church and other good causes said to me, "I get the greatest joy I have ever had in life by my giving. So many men with money are missing the biggest thrill of all by not giving." You and I may never give big sums, but if we are not having a vital part in the work of our church, we are missing one of life's highest satisfactions. Souls are to be won, lives are to be blessed, the Gospel is to be preached, missionaries must go to the ends of the earth with the Good News. Because of our gifts all these things can be done. Don't you want to have a part in this work? Let it be the right part — let it be God's part, and you will receive God's reward.

II. THE PROMISE IN THE TEXT IF WE PUT GOD FIRST

He says that "all these things" will be added unto us. What things? Jesus has just been talking about material things, so He is saying that if we put Him first, He will give us all we need. This is the word of a gentleman. We know that He will keep His promise. Why don't you test Him? The only thing that counts at the end of the way is what you have done for Jesus. I am pleading for you to lay up treasures in heaven, where thieves never steal, where market conditions will never affect you, where your treasures will bless you throughout eternity.

A certain man kept a lighthouse on a rugged coast. He had many ships and many lives in his keeping. On the first of each month an oil truck came and left him enough oil for that month. He was cautioned to guard his supply of oil carefully. One night there was a knock on his door. A woman asked for some oil to keep her child warm, and the man gave it to her. Then a man wanted enough oil so that his son could read at night. Then another man wanted some oil for his engine. Slowly the man parceled out the valuable oil. Toward the end of the month the oil gave out, and the light in the lighthouse went out. That night three ships went down and scores of lives were lost. The next morning the government agent was there, rebuking this careless man. The man began to apologize and tell about how he had given the oil away for good causes. But the government man said sternly, "You were given one task — to keep the light burning. You used the oil for secondary purposes, therefore ships went down and lives were lost. For this there is no excuse."

Dear friends, as Christians, we have one task above all others. We are to keep the light shining for Christ. We are to keep the light shining on this corner and around the world. We have just one little life. We have no right to exhaust that life on the world and then have nothing left for Christ and His church. So let's keep the light shining by giving our best to Jesus, remembering that He said, "Seek ye first the kingdom of God and his righteousness and all of these things shall be added unto you."

Sermon 7

WHO'S THAT KNOCKING AT MY HEART'S DOOR?

Revelation 3:20

Holman Hunt has painted a wonderful picture and given it the title, *The Light of the World*. In this picture we see Christ arrayed in royal robes, standing before a fast-closed door. In His left hand He holds a lighted lantern. With His right hand He is knocking upon the heavy door. But the door is bolted on the inside and no one comes to open it. That is the picture of the human heart. Jesus stands outside the door and knocks, but men will not let Him in because their hearts are filled with sin and worldliness. Finally Jesus turns sadly away and says, "Ye will not come unto me that ye might have everlasting life."

On the other hand we have the sweet promise that if we knock upon His door, He will open unto us. He has said, "Ask and ye shall receive, seek and ye shall find, knock and it shall be opened unto you." God is a seeking God. In Luke 19:10 we read, "The Son of man is come to seek and to save that which was lost." Yet here is the strange thing. Men run from the God who wants to bless them.

I. Who Is It That Knocks?

It is the Lord Jesus Christ, God's Only-begotten Son. He is the One who loves you most. He is the One who came to earth and suffered and died for you. He is the One who wants to give you His very best. He is the One who wants to take you to heaven at the end of the way. If the President of the United States or the Queen of England knocked at your door, you would consider it a great honor. You would surely invite them in. Yet this One who knocks at your heart's door is the Royal Guest from heaven. What folly to turn Him away!

II. Who Can Open the Door of Your Heart?

You are the only one who can open that door. Jesus Christ is a perfect gentleman. He will not force His way into your heart. He will never enter an unwelcome heart. It is true that men shut their hearts against Him. They go their way in the sin of this world and have nothing to do with this One who wants to come in and bring them the richest blessings that could be bestowed upon them. It is true that men shut their homes to Jesus. In many homes the Name of Christ is never mentioned, prayer is never offered, the blessing is never offered at the table. Yet Jesus wants to come into your home and make it a little colony of heaven down here on earth.

It is also true that some churches are shut against Jesus. Our text was written to the church at Laodicea. This church was neither hot nor cold. The members went through many forms and rituals, but Christ was left out. I would not be too critical of any church or group of churches, but I must say that Christ is not a living reality in many churches today. He is not in a church which doesn't preach Christ and Him crucified. He is not in a church which doesn't tell men that they are lost and need a Saviour.

Some years ago I was in New York City and decided to go and hear a prominent man preach. This man offered three prayers and preached a sermon which was about thirty minutes long. He never mentioned the Name of Christ in either of the prayers. In the sermon he quoted something that Jesus had said, in just about the same manner that I would quote from Shakespeare or Browning. I did not feel the presence of Christ in that church.

There is an old story about a country man who moved

Who's That Knocking at My Heart's Door? 69

to the city. He went to the city church on Sunday and told the pastor that he wanted to join that church. The pastor said, "Are you sure that you want to join our church?" And the man answered that he was sure. Then the pastor told him to go home and think about it and pray about it. The old man came back the next Sunday and again expressed his desire to join that church. The pastor asked him if he had prayed about it. The man answered, "Yes, I talked to the Lord about it and He said that He hoped I could get into this church. He said that He had been trying to get into it for many years and had not been able to do so." Yes, some churches are closed to Jesus.

III. How Does Christ Knock at the Heart's Door?

A. *He knocks through the conscience.* Your conscience tells you about your sin and your need of a Saviour. Look yonder into that garden just outside the city of Jerusalem. A man has just hanged himself and he is now lying dead upon the ground. That man is Judas. Why did he kill himself? What made him do it? He had betrayed Christ and his conscience had driven him to suicide.

In my first pastorate I baptized a seventy-year-old man one Sunday night. His two grown sons were baptized the same night. This man said to me, "In all the years that I have lived, I never did a wrong thing but that my conscience lashed me and told me that it was wrong." Yes, Jesus knocks at the heart's door through the conscience.

B. *He knocks through the Gospel.* Paul said, "I am not ashamed of the gospel of Christ, for it is the power of God unto salvation to every one that believeth." The true Gospel has never lost its power. If we could have a mighty sweep of old-time gospel preaching throughout the land, I believe that it would result in a real revival. In the first days of my ministry I was preaching in a revival in a country church. On the last day of the meeting they were taking up an offering for him. A young man who had been saved in the meeting came to him and said, "I am very sorry that I do not have any money to put into the offering, but I want you to know that I will be forever grateful to you. I will never forget the sermons that you preached here in the church. These sermons led me to accept Jesus Christ as my Saviour." It was the Gospel that did it, empowered by the Spirit of God.

One night in another meeting the pastor had supper in a certain home. The wife and mother in that home said to him, "I am so glad that you are here, helping us in our revival meeting. My husband is away at this time, but he will be home Saturday. He will be at church Saturday night. He is not saved. I am praying that your sermon on Saturday night will touch his heart and lead him to Christ." On Saturday night when the invitation was given after the sermon, this big man came down the aisle to make his surrender to the Lord Jesus Christ. It was the Gospel that did it, empowered by the Spirit of God. Sometime ago I preached to a church that was packed with people. At the close of the service a man came forward to accept Christ as His Saviour. As he took my hand he said, "You were preaching to me alone tonight. I have come to give my heart to the Saviour." I did not know the man or anything about him. It was the Gospel that did it, empowered by the Spirit of God. Yes, Christ knocks through the Gospel.

C. *He knocks through a good life*. After a certain man had been saved the preacher said to him, "What was it in my sermon that led you to give your heart to Christ?"

The man said, "It was nothing in your sermon. It was the faithful consecrated Christian life that my wife has lived down through the years which made me know that I needed her Saviour."

Some senators were discussing religion in the senate dining room one day. When one man defended the Christian religion, another one said to him, "Senator, you surely don't believe in that old-time stuff about being born again, do you?"

And the senator replied, "I am sorry to say that I am not a Christian, but a year ago my wife and daughter attended a revival meeting and then told me that they had been saved. Their lives have been so wonderful and so different since that time, that I know there must be something to the Christian religion." Oh, I wish that all of us lived such Christlike lives that the world could see the reality of our religion and want Christ to be their Saviour.

I know some men who are not Christians, but whose wives are professing Christians and church members. These women say that they would like to see their husbands saved, yet their own lives do not measure up. They neglect church attendance and put many other things before the Lord. They go to the same places their husbands go and do the same things that their husbands do. The husbands can easily see that their religion doesn't mean much to them. They see no difference in their lives and the lives of their wives, therefore they are not made to feel their own need of a Saviour. Christ can use our lives to knock on the door of sinful hearts if we will but live rightly for Him.

D. *He knocks through the sorrows of life.* A prominent man died in our city some months ago. Several years ago I was in a revival meeting in Roswell, New Mexico. This man's wife died and they called me over long distance asking me to return for the funeral service. Since I was conducting two services a day in the meeting up there, I didn't see how I could make the trip. But this man came to the phone and sobbed out his heart to me. He told me that he would send a private plane in which I could make the trip. He said that his wife's dying request was that I should conduct her funeral. I did come back to the city and conducted the funeral service. At that time this man was not a Christian. Sometime later I began to visit him in his home and talk to him about the Saviour. Each time I would visit him I would find him with a New Testament in his hand. He began to attend church every Sunday, and one Sunday morning he walked down the aisle and gave his heart to the Saviour. I baptized him that night. He became a devoted Christian before he died. But his interest in his salvation began when a sorrow came to him.

In a meeting which I held in a country church a middle-aged man was gloriously saved. Before that time he had shown no interest in Christianity. That was when we had running boards on automobiles. One day this man was driving through the woods and his ten-year-old boy was standing on the runningboard. He drove rapidly around a curve and the boy was thrown against a tree and killed. This tragedy and sorrow brought this man to realize his need of a Saviour and caused him to seek the Lord's salvation.

Sometimes God must break our hearts to win us to Him, but certainly that's much better than letting us go on to hell.

E. *He knocks through His Spirit.* A sinner comes to a church service and during that service he begins to feel the weight of his sin. There is a strange tug at his heart and this is caused by the Holy Spirit. A little girl came to see me sometime ago and said, "I want to be a Christian. Several times when you have preached and given the invitation, I felt something in my heart which made me want to go forward and accept Christ."

I said to her, "Who do you think it was that made you feel this way?"

She replied simply, "It was God." Yes, it was God, the Holy Spirit. Jesus said that He would do exactly this thing when He came into the world. Christ knocks at the heart's door through the pleadings of the Spirit of God.

But here is the tragic thing — men hear Jesus knocking at the heart's door, yet they turn Him away. They feel the convicting power of the Holy Spirit, they realize their need

Who's That Knocking at My Heart's Door? 73

of a Saviour, but they go back into the world and are lost forever.

IV. Why Won't Men Let Jesus In?

There is one answer — sin. Anything that keeps you from Jesus is sin. Yet we must know that sin can never permanently satisfy and that it damns the soul forever.

V. What Happens When We Let Jesus Into Our Hearts?

He says that He will come in and sup with us and that we will sup with Him. Ah, yes, when Jesus comes He brings a feast of good things into your heart! Every person who has ever accepted Christ can testify that He brings peace and joy and happiness that nothing else in this world can ever give. When I was pastor of the Broadway Baptist Church in Knoxville, Tennessee, a certain man ran a grocery store just across the street from the church. This man had been to our church once or twice, so I went over to see him one day. While he was handling an order of groceries, I talked to him about the Lord Jesus Christ. He came to church again the next Sunday night and gave his heart to the Saviour. Some weeks later I visited him on a Sunday afternoon. He was in the backyard, flying a kite for his little girl. When I went out into the backyard, he pulled in the kite and we walked toward the house. I asked him how he felt since he had become a Christian. He said to me, "I never knew that life could be so sweet and so wonderful." That man is now a deacon and treasurer of that church. There is no feeling in all the world to compare with the feeling that comes to one who has just found Christ as Saviour and Lord. Do you want joy? Then take Jesus. Do you want salvation? Then take the Saviour. Do you want the music of heaven in your soul? Then you must take the Master Musician of heaven. Do you want heaven? Then you must take Him.

A little boy was reading from the Book of Revelation at the family altar. When he came to the part about Jesus knocking at the door, he said to his father, "Daddy, did they let Him in?" One day life's little journey will be over for you. The days of opportunity will be gone. You will be lying in a casket and someone will ask, "Did he let Jesus in?" Oh, it will be glorious if it can be said of you, "Yes, when Jesus knocked at his heart's door he let Him in and he was saved." It will be tragic if someone must say, "No, he wouldn't let Him in and now it's too late." Christ is knocking at the door now. Your decision will bless or curse you throughout eternity.

Christ tells of the foolish virgins who waited too late to buy oil for their lamps. When they came back to enter the room where the wedding supper was being held we read that "the door was shut." They had waited too long. Noah preached repentance for one hundred and twenty years. Men laughed at his warnings, but when the flood came surely many of them must have pounded upon the door of the ark, crying out for entrance. But it was too late. God had shut the door and no man could open it.

I heard of a woman who was reared in a Primitive Baptist influence. She felt that if God was going to save her, He would do it regardless of what she did. On her death bed she said to her daughter, "All these years Christ has been knocking at the door of my heart. I felt it, but I wouldn't let Him in and now it's too late." People ought not to die like that. He is knocking at your heart today, why not let Him in?

During the Civil War a Quaker father went out upon a battlefield looking for his son who had been wounded. On every side he heard the groans of the wounded and the dying, but he couldn't locate his son. Finally, he lifted up his voice and in his quaint Quaker way he cried out, "John Hardin, thy father is calling for thee." He repeated this cry over and over again.

Finally, he heard a faint voice in the distance saying, "Here, Father, here I am."

Jesus stands today upon the battlefield of life. He says, "I am calling for thee, I love thee, I died for thee, I want to save thee. Come unto Me, all ye that labor and are heavy laden and I will give you rest." Won't you say, "Here I am, Jesus. I will be yours forever"?

Sermon 8

PAUL'S KNOWS

II Timothy 1:12; Romans 8:28; II Corinthians 5:1

In 1895 a New York preacher preached a sermon about the fast living of his day. He talked about the bicycle craze and said, "This speed is not good for us. It will develop a generation of nervous and high-strung creatures." A few years later the automobile came along. The first cars ran fifteen miles per hour. Many prominent doctors said that this was a dangerous speed and would result in heart failure for many people. But today our cars run eighty and ninety miles an hour and we ride on planes at five and six hundred miles per hour and think nothing of it.

But the preacher of 1895 was right in one way — we are living at a rapid pace. Life is a question of doing something fast and getting somewhere in a hurry. We are nervous and anxious and restless. Medical men tell us that there is more mental suffering today than physical suffering. Thousands of hospital beds are filled with mental cases. As you walk the streets of our cities and look into the faces of our people, you cannot help but notice that the multitudes are marked by anxiety and worry.

But there is something worse today. Many people are afflicted with religious unrest. We have new isms and cults on every side. Men are seeking something to satisfy the unrest in their hearts. They are turning to religions which are not founded upon the Word of God. These religions cannot satisfy the human heart. But I know where souls can find rest, where hearts can find peace and where lives can find satisfaction. Jesus Christ still holds all that the world needs.

Paul's Knows

> I heard the voice of Jesus say,
> "Come unto Me and rest;
> Lay down, thou weary one,
> Lay down thy head upon My breast."
>
> I came to Jesus as I was,
> Weary and worn and sad,
> I found in Him a resting place,
> And He has made me glad.

Christianity gives you something to hold on to. While others doubt and say, "I don't know," the child of God can say, "I know." Paul said it long ago and you and I can say it today. The man who follows Christ has an anchor safe and sure. His faith lifts him up above all the unrest of the world. Paul said, "I know" three times. So let us look at Paul's "knows."

I. "I KNOW WHOM I HAVE BELIEVED, AND AM PERSUADED THAT HE IS ABLE TO KEEP THAT WHICH I HAVE COMMITTED UNTO HIM AGAINST THAT DAY."

We pass by the man who guesses, and listen to the man who knows. When you are sick, you don't want to listen to a doctor who is a quack, but you want a man who really knows something about your condition and what to do about it. If you want to know something about an airplane, you don't ask the man who never saw one, but you ask the man who knows all about them. Now Paul, the greatest Christian, says, "I know." Therefore, we stop and listen. He had had an experience with Christ. He had talked with Him. He had walked with Him. He had been filled with His Spirit. He knew what he was talking about.

Often in quoting this verse, someone says, "I know *in* whom I have believed." This is incorrect. The verse says, "I know whom I have believed," and the "whom" stands for Christ. Someone has well said that they don't want even a preposition to come between them and Christ. If you have been really and truly saved you can say, "I know Christ," not "I know about Christ." The saved man knows a Person, One who came into his heart, One who forgave his sins, One who walks with him and keeps him and blesses him. You may guess about many things. You may not understand all of the Bible, but how wonderful it is to be able to say, "I know Christ. I met Him one day face to face. I fell in love with Him. Now I am His and He is mine."

Mel Trotter was once asked how he knew that he was saved and he replied, "I was there when it happened."

When Sir James Simpson, the great scientist who made many discoveries, was asked what he considered his greatest discovery, he said, "My greatest discovery was when I learned that I was a sinner, and took Jesus Christ as my Saviour." Some years ago an unsaved friend of mine attended a revival under a Texas brush arbor. Being convicted for his sin and burdened for his salvation, he lingered at the brush arbor long after the service was ended, talking and praying with the preacher. He was gloriously saved that night. He then mounted his horse and rode home, shouting as he went down the highway. As he passed the homes of those who knew him, they could hear his shouting and they said, "That's Arthur Giles. He was saved tonight."

Later on he said to me, "The years have gone by since that night, but I have never forgotten that experience. When the doubts come I always go back to that hour and I am comforted in remembering that I met Christ and that I belong to Him. With such memories I defeat my doubts and whip the devil."

Now everyone can know Jesus. Everyone can have this wonderful salvation. If you want to meet a man, what do you do? You go up to him and say, "I want to meet you." Do you want to meet Jesus? Then come to Him right now. Bring your sins and lay them upon Him. Trust Him with all of your heart. He will become your best friend. It is not given to all of us to know the kings and the great men of the earth, but everyone can know Jesus.

A young nobleman walked out of his palace one cold morning. He met a beggar who was cold and hungry, and reached in his pocket for a coin to give this beggar. He found that his pockets were empty, so he simply said, "I am sorry, but I have nothing for you this morning, my brother."

An hour later when he returned that way the beggar said to him, "Thank you, sir."

The nobleman said, "Why do you thank me? I did nothing for you."

"Yes," said the beggar, "you called me brother and that brightened the whole day for me."

My friend, Jesus does more than that for us. He calls us brothers and sisters and then gives us all the true riches of heaven and earth. Do your sins overcome you? Do doubts often fill your heart? Then that's the time to say, "Back yonder I found Christ as my Saviour. I know that I am saved. He said that if I came to Him He would not cast me out. He said that if I would receive Him, He would give me power to become a son of God. Now I know that I am His child and all the devils in hell cannot shake that fact."

One day a lady saw a butterfly inside of the house, flying around a picture window. On the outside a bird was pecking at the window and the butterfly became greatly frightened. "Oh, little butterfly," said the woman, "you are just as safe as if that bird were a hundred miles away." And so if you and I are in Christ we are on the inside. Satan may try to get to us and take us to hell, but Christ is between us and Satan, therefore we are safe. We can say with Paul, "I know whom I have believed, and am persuaded that He is able to keep that which I have committed unto Him against that day."

II. "We Know That All Things Work Together for Good to Them That Love God, to Them Who Are the Called According to His Purpose."

Again Paul speaks out of his experience. He had been beaten, he had been put in prison, he had been persecuted, he had been shipwrecked, but he was able to say, "It all worked out for my good." On another day he said, "All of this has turned out for the furtherance of the Gospel." It doesn't matter what we must endure, if the end result brings glory to God and blessing to someone else and salvation to souls.

Now it often seems that this text is untrue. Hardships and troubles come to us and we say, "This can't be good — I am suffering too much." But the years pass by and God works out His purpose and one day we can say, "That was the best thing that ever happened to me." The text does not say that all things are good, but it does say that when God puts all these things together and works them out, they do turn out for our good.

In the early days of my ministry I was invited to preach one Sunday at a church which did not have a pastor. I preached that day and we had good services and I greatly enjoyed the fellowship with the good people in that town. Deep down in my heart I was hoping that this church would call me to be its pastor. Two weeks later, I was invited to come back and preach again and then I was quite sure that they were interested in me and would extend me a call. On that Sunday night after church the good ladies of the church said to me, "We want you to be our pastor. We are going to clean up the pastorium so that you and your family can move in right away." The Chairman of the Pulpit Committee talked the matter over with me and told me that the church would have a business meeting on the following Wednesday night and extend this call. I was delighted and looked forward to moving to that town and serving as pastor of that church. However, on Wednesday night there was a heavy downpour of rain and the church leaders who came to church that night felt that they should wait until they could have a larger congregation before extending a definite call. Before this could be done, these people began to think further about the matter and wrote me that they felt I was too young and inexperienced to take on the responsibilities of that pastorate. I was greatly disappointed and heartbroken. However, the Lord worked out things for me in such a wonderful way that in later years when I rode through that town, I would thank God that I had not been called to that pastorate. I came to learn the truth of the text. I know that God was making all things work together for my good.

Some years ago I had a young dentist and his wife as members of the church where I was serving as pastor. They were happily looking forward to the coming of their first baby. The husband had already taken out insurance for the baby and the mother had lovingly prepared the sweet little garments that the baby was to wear. However, the baby lived just a few minutes after birth. I went to the hospital and talked to the young couple and I quoted this text. I told them that all things work together for good to those who love the Lord. The woman cried out, "I can't see it. How can this be a good thing?" But a year or two later another baby was born to this couple. This baby was beautiful and healthy, and brought supreme happiness to the young father and mother. They came at last to see the truth of this text.

A freight car was parked in the railroad yards and a mother bird built her nest in the car, laid her eggs and several little baby birds hatched. Then the time came for the car to be moved. This would necessarily have broken up the nest. But someone wrote to the superintendent and he took the car out of service until the birds could fly away. Oh, if a great railroad system would protect a little brood of birds, surely a great God will take care of us and make all things work together for our good! Yes, "His eye is on the sparrow and I know He watches me."

It's a sin for us to worry as we do. Jesus said, "Be not anxious." But we disobey Him and worry ourselves sick. Yet God has promised to look after us if we look after His interests. "Seek ye first the kingdom of God and his righteousness, and all these things shall be added unto you." The psalmist wrote out of long experience when he said, "I have been young but now I am old, yet I have never seen the righteous forsaken, nor his seed begging bread."

So when trouble comes, when it seems that the whole world is against you, just remember that "all things work together for good to them that love God."

III. "WE KNOW THAT IF OUR EARTHLY HOUSE OF THIS TABERNACLE WERE DISSOLVED, WE HAVE A BUILDING OF GOD, AN HOUSE NOT MADE WITH HANDS, ETERNAL IN THE HEAVENS."

Isn't that wonderful? Every day our bodies are decaying. Every day they are getting older and weaker. But Paul said, "That's all right, just rest in this great fact — when this body is gone, God will give us a better one. He will give us a body not made with hands, eternal in the heavens." Paul never speculated about the matter of eternal life. He said that for him it would be "better to depart and be with Christ," yet he cheerfully remained in the world and went on with his work. He knew that one day his head would be placed upon a block, the axe would fall and his head would roll off the block. But he also knew that his soul, his spirit, the real Paul, would soar up into the heavens to be with God.

The Bishop of London one day visited a dying child. Since she was frightened about the matter of death, he tried to soothe and comfort her. He said to her, "Would you be afraid if I took you up in my arms and carried you into the next room?"

She replied that she would not be afraid.

"Well," said the bishop, "someone ten thousand times kinder and stronger than I am is going to do just that for you. That's all that death is. Heaven is as close to you as the next room and Christ is as near to you as I am." The little child was comforted by these words. Oh, if we live in close fellowship with Christ, heaven will never be very far away!

When Charles Kingsley lay dying he cried aloud, "How beautiful God is." Napoleon once visited an art gallery and looked at some of Raphael's paintings. The attendant said to him, "These pictures are immortal." Napoleon asked, "How long do you think they will last?" When the attendant said that he thought they would last at least five hundred years, Napoleon said in a sarcastic vein, "A beautiful immortality that is." Ah, yes, immortality is longer than that. Our eternal home will last much longer than that.

One day God took Moses up to the top of a high mountain. He showed him all the beauties of the Promised Land, but had to say to him, "Moses, you can't enter the Promised Land." The tears must have flowed down the cheeks of the old partiarch, but God put His arm around his shoulder and said, "Moses, I have something better for you than that. I am going to take you up to live with Me in My home." And Moses has been there ever since. Yes, God gives us a house here, but it is just for a little while. He is preparing one better for us on the other side of the river.

The express agent in Knoxville, Tennessee, was one of my deacons. He told me that he was going to release a cage of homing pigeons at dawn one morning and asked me to go along with him. We went down to the station and a cage of pigeons was brought out onto the platform. When this man opened the cage the pigeons flew straight up into the air, circled the station a couple of times and then headed due north. Later in the day he received a wire stating that every one of these pigeons had landed safely in the home loft in the state of Ohio. God put the homing instinct into these pigeons and He also puts that instinct into the human soul. We long for a life after this life and an eternal home where cares and sorrows can never touch us. And God in His love and mercy has provided these things for all who accept His Son. Someday our earthly house will fall. Someday the school of life will be over. The day of trouble will be done. Then God will open the door and we shall be forever with the Lord.

We can, therefore, say with Paul, "I know that I am saved. I know that God is caring for me. I know that He has prepared a happy home for me just beyond the sunset." God takes care of the past, the present and the future. He takes care of the past when He forgives our sin. He takes care of the present as He cares for us every day. He takes care of the future by preparing a place in glory for us. Earthly joys may fade away, but if we can say, "I am saved, God is caring for me, there is a heavenly home waiting for me," that is enough to make us shout for joy.

It is Christmastime. Three little girls were looking into a show window, and a man nearby listened to their conversation. Two of the girls were describing everything in the window to a third girl. They told her about the dolls, the trains, the teddy bears. You see, the third little girl was blind. The man who was looking on said to himself, "It's no use, girls, you will never be able to describe all the beauty and color in that wonderful window." I feel the same way when I try to tell you of Jesus and heaven. No matter how long I preached, I could never tell you how wonderful they are.

But suppose that this man could have given sight to that little girl. And suppose that he had taken them into the store and bought all these things for the three little girls. That would have been a picture of what Jesus will do for us someday. All the earthly scales will fall from our eyes, we shall see Him as He is, and the treasures of heaven will be ours. Sinner, don't you want that? Don't you want Him to forgive you and transform you and give you peace and hope? Christian, don't you love Him? Then come and serve Him better in the future than you have in the past.

Sermon 9

THE END OF THE TRAIL
(Part One)

II Timothy 4:6-8

There never has been a greater man of God upon the earth than the Apostle Paul. He went all out for Christ. From the day that he met his Saviour on the Damascus Road until the day that he met death at the hands of the Roman executioner, he gave his best in faithful service to God. Before his conversion he used all the powers and talents of his great life against Christ and His cause. After his conversion he gave all the powers and talents of that life to Christ. He loved Christ as probably no man ever loved Him. He served Christ more faithfully than any man ever served Him. He suffered more for Christ than any man who ever lived. He probably won more people to Christ and established more churches and wielded a greater influence for the Lord than any other Christian who ever existed.

Now he is coming to the end of the trail. He knows that death is near. No more long journeys through summer's heat or winter's cold. No more imprisonment, no more beatings, no more stonings, no more hardships, no more suffering. The journey of life will soon be over and he will be at home with the Christ whom he loved above all else. And where is he now as he faces death? Not upon a downy couch in some palace of luxury — not upon a hospital bed surrounded by sympathetic doctors and nurses. No, he is in a cold, damp prison cell, far from home, far from loved ones, far from friends. On the outside of the

The End of the Trail (Part One)

prison the block is ready where he will soon place his head. The axe is sharp that will soon be raised. The executioner is ready to do his dirty work.

Do you feel sorry for the poor old preacher? Don't do it! That cell is aglow with heavenly light. Paul is radiantly happy. He knows that to die will be gain for him. He knows that he will soon be released from all earthly sorrows, he knows that he will soon see his Saviour.

The falcon is a bird held to the master's wrist by a chain. Just as soon as he is released, he soars upward toward the sky. So Paul was just waiting for his soul to be released, that he might go up to be with Jesus forever. And listen to his triumphant words as he waits, "For I am now ready to be offered and the time of my departure is at hand. I have fought a good fight, I have finished my course, I have kept the faith: henceforth there is laid up for me a crown of righteousness, which the Lord, the righteous judge shall give be at that day: and not to me only, but unto all them also that love His appearing."

In this and the next chapter I want you to see three things: The Consummation, The Conqueror, The Crown.

I. THE CONSUMMATION

Paul said, "I am now ready to be offered." He knew that his time had come and he had no fear. Death to the faithful Christian is not a monster. He doesn't think of a chilly river nor a dark valley. He rejoices to go out and meet his Saviour and receive his reward. D. L. Moody often said, "One day you will read in the papers that D. L. Moody is dead. Don't you believe it! I will be more alive than ever before." When he came to the end of the way, he said, "Earth is receding, heaven is descending, God is calling and I am going home." A little later he said, "Is this death? It is not bad — it is glorious. This is my coronation day!"

Why could Paul say, "I am now ready to be offered"?

Was it because he had worked so hard for Christ? Was it because he suffered so much? Was it because he had preached so often? Was it because he had won so many souls or established so many churches? No, these are not the things that save a man. These are not the things that prepare him for death. He was ready because long ago he had met the Son of God on the Damascus Road, and had repented of his sins and put all of his faith in the Saviour. Everywhere he went he told people that he had been saved through repentance and faith, and told everyone that they must be saved in the same way. There is only one way of salvation.

What then do our works have to do with our salvation? They have nothing to do with our salvation, but they have everything to do with our rewards. We are saved by the grace of God when we turn from our sins and trust Christ as our Saviour. We are rewarded at the end of the way because of our works for Him.

Just imagine that I am a wealthy man and that I own a steamship as large and palatial as the *Queen Mary*. And suppose that I offered you a free trip to Europe on this ship. You would accept the invitation and get on board the ship and begin to enjoy the voyage. Then suppose that a day out from port I came to you and said, "I need some help in the purser's office. Would you mind working down there for me an hour or two a day?"

You would say, "Yes, I will be glad to help you in that way." You then work each day in the purser's office and when we get to Europe I hand you a check for a hundred dollars. You would then say to me, "Why are you giving me this money?"

I would say, "I am paying you for the work that you did in the purser's office."

But you would answer, "I don't expect any pay for that work. You gave me a free trip on your ship." Then I would say, "Yes, I gave you a free trip over on the ship, but since

The End of the Trail (Part One)

you worked on the way, I am giving you this money as an extra reward." Well, in like manner, Christ has promised to take us to heaven if we would put our trust in Him. However, if we work for Him on the way to heaven, He will have a reward waiting for us when we get there.

A good Christian man lay dying and a friend said to him, "Have you made your peace with God?"

The man answered, "No, I don't have to do that. Nineteen hundred years ago on Calvary Christ made peace with God for me. I entered into that peace when I trusted Him as my Saviour. I have no fears now, I am ready to die." Paul had that peace in his heart and now he was ready to go. Do you have that peace? Do you know that it is all well with your soul? If tomorrow were your day to go and you knew it, could you say, "It is well with my soul"? If you can't say that, the same Saviour who took Paul home is ready to save you today. He will give you the peace that passeth all understanding and prepare you for death.

Paul pictures his death as a departure. He said, "The time of my departure is at hand." We have a picture here of a ship. The passengers are all on board, the gangplank has been lifted, the whistle has blown and the ship is just ready to leave the dock. But when a ship leaves one place, you expect it to land soon in another place. In 1959 we boarded a ship in San Francisco. As it pulled out of the harbor the crowds were waving, the music was playing, and some people were even shedding tears. But we who were on the ship expected to land soon in another place. Four and a half days later our ship pulled into the harbor at Honolulu. The bands were playing, the crowds were cheering and and our friends were there to meet us. So when we depart from this life others may weep, but we can rejoice because, with Christ in our hearts, we hope soon to land in heaven amid the shouts of the redeemed and the songs of the angelic hosts.

Look yonder into that Roman prison cell. It may be

physically dark, but there is light at eventide for this old soldier of the cross. So he says, "I am now ready to be offered, and the time of my departure is at hand."

II. The Conqueror

We are told often that when one faces death his whole life passes in review. In that hour some rejoice over a life well-lived for Christ. Others cry out for an opportunity to go back and live life over again, so that they might live it differently. I am afraid that many of you who are giving your lives to the world now and who are not giving Christ first place, are going to have an awful time of remorse and sorrow when you come to the end of the way. But Paul looked back and was satisfied. He didn't have to look back to the other side of his conversion experience — that was all under the blood of Christ. But as he looked over his life since conversion, he had no reason to be ashamed.

First, he said that he had "fought a good fight." The Christian life is a warfare — we are always fighting. Now we are told that this fight is not against physical forces, but against the spiritual powers of Satan on every side. And the reason that so many people are defeated is because they go into the battle empty-handed. They try to fight these battles alone, instead of taking Christ with them. Today there is a great struggle going on in the world. On one side we find Satan and all of his forces. On the other side we find Christ and all of His forces. We make the decision about whose army we are going to fight in. If we get on the winning side it will mean everything here and hereafter. If we are on the losing side it will mean defeat here and everlasting sorrow and death hereafter.

Now in this warfare you fight against your own carnal nature. Read the seventh chapter of Romans and see if this is not a picture of the eternal fight which goes on within you — the fight between good and evil. When you become a Christian God gives you a new spiritual nature, but He

The End of the Trail (Part One)

doesn't take away the old carnal nature. The flesh is still with you and always the fight will be going on between the flesh and the spirit. The spiritual nature says, "You are a Christian — you must not do this thing." The carnal nature says, "Go ahead. This won't harm you. You will enjoy it." The carnal nature says, "Give into this thing." The spiritual nature says, "Give in to God." If you don't have a constant battle between the good and the evil, it is not because you are perfect — it is because you have given in to sin.

How is the battle over the carnal nature won? It will never be completely won until you lay aside the robe of flesh and mount up to the skies. But you can often overcome through a life of prayer, a life of self-denial, a life of active service, a life of close communion with Christ.

Then we must fight against worldliness. What is worldliness? It is anything that comes between you and God — anything that keeps you from living your best for God.

Paul had a young man named Demas who went around with him and helped him in his evangelistic meetings. But Demas fell by the wayside. Paul said, "Demas hath forsaken me, having loved this present world." And every pastor can say, as he looks over his church roll, "Here is one who used to be faithful. He was here every time the church doors were open. He served God well. He tithed. He loved the Lord. But where is he now? He has forsaken me and the church and the Lord. He has loved the world and gone back to it." But what does the Bible say? "Love not the world, neither the things that are in the world, for he that loveth the world, the love of the Father is not in him."

One day someone comes to you representing an organization of the world, an organization which does nothing to win souls or bring glory to God. You are offered a position which will mean glamor and prestige and popularity and publicity. But at the same time this means that you will be forced to give less time and less effort to Christ and your church. What must you do? You must fight it. You must put it aside. You must say, "Nothing, absolutely nothing must ever come between me and my best for Christ."

A certain young woman had an unusual talent for playing the violin. She was in great demand at the dances which were held in her community. She was not a Christian. One night she had no other engagement, so she went to a revival meeting and heard the Gospel. She saw herself as a lost sinner. She was deeply convicted by the Spirit of God. She went forward and confessed Christ as her Saviour. The next night she came back to church. She felt that she hadn't done enough just to accept Christ as her Saviour, so she brought her beloved violin and laid it upon the altar. She was simply saying that she was not only willing for Christ to save her, but that she wanted her life and talent dedicated to His service. She never used the violin again except in a way that would bless someone.

Our churches are full of people who are perfectly willing for Christ to save them and take them to heaven at the end of their way. That is the extent of their Christianity. They are not giving Christ their time and talents and service. They are giving these to the world. You can never say at the end of the way, "I have fought a good fight," unless you have turned down the world in favor of Jesus Christ.

Often also as Christians we must fight against our associates. I do not mean by this that we are to be obnoxious in our relationships to others. I do mean, however, that we must often take a stand opposite to those around us. Sometimes these associates are those who would draw you away from Christ. They first plan something to keep one away from church — then they draw one into something which is questionable — then they draw one into sin. This is something which we must continually fight against. The

The End of the Trail (Part One)

way to do it is to remain always one hundred per cent faithful to Christ and His church and never compromise your Christian convictions.

Then the Christian must sometimes fight for the true Gospel. We are living today in an age of cults and isms. The world is full of man-made religions which have no Bible foundation. These religions have many champions trying to win converts. When they come to us we must say, "Here is a Bible, it is the inerrant Word of God. Show me the truth as you find it here and I will follow the truth. Otherwise I will have nothing to do with your doctrine."

Yes, Paul fought a good fight. He lived a stormy life. Often wicked men sought to kill him, but he had the sweet peace of God on the inside. Looking back now he has no regrets. At the end of the way the businessman looks back over his life, remembers the good deals he made, the profits that he enjoyed, and smiles with satisfaction. The lawyer looks back and remembers the great cases that he has pled and won. He remembers the men he has saved from prison and death and he has joy in the memories. The physician looks back and thinks of the operations he has performed. He thinks of the treatments he has given and the grateful thanks of those whose lives he has saved. Remembering all of this, his heart is filled with great satisfaction. As the Christian comes to the end of the trail, and looks back, he remembers that all that counts then is his relationship to Christ and the service he has given to Him. What kind of memories are you building up? What are you doing that will bring joy at the end of the way?

I want to tell you that Christ makes all the difference in the world. He makes the difference in the life here and the life hereafter. So if you want joy at the end of life's long road, give Him first place in your heart.

A soldier said to a chaplain, "You say that all men are made in the image of God. In the war I saw some men behave worse than animals — on the other hand, I saw some who gave their lives for others in sacrificial service. How do you account for the difference?"

The chaplain was wise enough to say, "Christ makes the difference." And He does — He makes all the difference in the world. Surely at the end of the way that difference stands out more prominently than ever.

A little boy was making the long train trip from New York to the West Coast. From time to time the kind people on the train would talk to him and try to make his trip more comfortable and more enjoyable. One day someone said to him, "Aren't you tired?" "Oh, yes," he said, "but my father is going to meet me at the end of the way." The next day another said to him, "Aren't you lonely?" The boy answered, "Yes, but my father is going to meet me at the end of the way." Finally the train rolled into a California station. The boy jumped off the train and into the loving arms of a loving father.

As it was for Paul, so life for us is a struggle. Often we are tired, often we are lonely, often we are hurt. But God, the great Heavenly Father, is waiting at the end of the way. When we see Him we will forget all the toils of the road. God help us to put our trust in Christ and follow Him, so that at the end of the way we can say, "I am now ready and the time of my departure is at hand. Christ is waiting to receive me."

Sermon 10

THE END OF THE TRAIL
(Part Two)

II Timothy 4:6-8

In the last chapter we saw Paul, the mighty minister of the Master, as he sat in his cell in a Roman prison. He knows that death is near — he will soon be martyred by the Roman executioner. So he writes his last letter, a letter to his beloved son in the ministry, Timothy. In his farewell words he voices some of the most cheerful sentiments ever expressed by a man who faces certain death. Let us hear them once again.

"For I am now ready to be offered, and the time of my departure is at hand. I have fought a good fight, I have finished my course, I have kept the faith: Henceforth there is laid up for me a crown of righteousness, which the Lord, the righteous judge, shall give me at that day, and not to me only, but unto all them also that love His appearing" (II Timothy 4:6-8).

In the previous chapter I spoke of Paul's readiness to be offered up — his eager desire to depart and be with Christ. I also spoke of the victorious feeling which filled his heart as he looked back over the long years. He said, "I have fought a good fight." He was not ashamed of the part he had played in the warfare of life. He had valiantly fought for the cause of Christ and he had been the victorious and happy conqueror. Now let us continue our thoughts about the valedictory address of this great warrior of the cross.

I. WE ARE STILL THINKING OF HIM AS A CONQUEROR

Paul says, "I have finished my course." We have seen Paul as a soldier, now we see him as an athlete. A battle is fought for victory — a race is run for reward. So Paul here is saying, "I have been running the Christian race for Christ, looking forward to the reward He has promised to all who serve Him." Paul evidently had seen the Olympic games in Greece. He knew that a man had to be a citizen of Greece before he could compete for the prizes in the race. Likewise, no one can compete for the rewards in the Christian race unless he has become a citizen of the Kingdom of Heaven. Paul met this requirement. Back on the Damascus Road he had found Christ and had become a citizen of His Kingdom. He had the right to run the race where Christ rewards the runners.

There are men today who know not Christ, yet they are doing good works and giving of their wealth, hoping for a reward at the end of the way. They are going to be greatly disappointed. Their works will perish with them. The only reward for anyone at the end of the way will be given to those who knew Christ and ran the race under His banner. We are saved by grace through faith. Just nail that great truth down and remember it. But, if after we have been saved we serve Christ faithfully, a reward is waiting for us at the end of the trail.

Then Paul knew that if he won the race he must strip off all unnecessary weight. A racer could run, wearing heavy boots and a big overcoat, but he would not be likely to win any race. So Paul says, "Let us lay aside every weight and the sin which doth so easily beset us, and let us run with patience the race that is set before us."

Oh, what a message for twentieth century Christians! We are trying to run a race for Christ, but we are so heavily laden with things of this world that we can't run very well. I know Christianity is not simply a matter of giving up something, but we can never be the Christians we ought

The End of the Trail (Part Two)

to be until we can say, "No," to the many calls of the world. Paul tells us to forget the things which are behind and press forward for Christ. Too many of us are remembering past triumphs, past experiences, past sorrows, and living on them. Oh, today we need to forget yesterday! We need to reach out for a fresh touch with God and then press on in the race.

I would like to ask you a personal question — won't you please think about it? What is that heavy thing which is keeping you from being the best Christian possible and serving Him in the finest way possible? Is it some secret sin? Is it a hot temper and a nasty disposition? Is it a connection with some worldly organization which saps your strength and consumes your time? Is it your bad feeling toward someone else? Is it plain laziness? Is it a critical attitude? Is it indifference and neglect? Even as a runner throws off the things which hold him back, why don't you, for Christ's sake, put those things aside and get into the Christian race as you should?

Now Paul's course was not an easy one. Hardships confronted him everywhere. He was often in prison, often beaten, often cold and hungry. He lost all things which we hold dear — family, home, friends. Wherever he went he got into trouble for Christ's sake. But he didn't quit — he kept on. One of the tragedies of our churches today is the fact that we have so many quitters. They start coming to church every Sunday and then quit. They start tithing and then quit. They start teaching a class and then quit. They start singing in the choir and then quit. Thank God, Jesus never quit. He went all the way to the cross for you and me. What a shame that we are not willing to give Him a little of our time and talent and all of our tithe!

We notice, also, that wherever Paul's course led him, he was faithful. They put him in the Philippian jail and he came out with a prison door under one arm and the jailer under the other, bringing him to Christ. They put him in a Roman jail and he won a runaway slave to Jesus Christ. They put him in Caesar's cell and soon Caesar's household was filled with Christians. We need to be faithful witnesses wherever we are, regardless of the circumstances. It isn't enough to be faithful within the four walls of the church, but our witness for Christ must be on a twenty-four hour basis. We are to be instant in season and out of season. We are to be faithful night and day, wherever we are, whatever we are doing.

And who was Paul's inspiration? Who was the One waiting to give him a crown at the end of the way? It was Jesus. Paul said that he was "looking unto Jesus, the Author and Finisher of our faith." Again he said, "I have had lots of trouble and there is more coming. But I am not worried, just so I can finish my course with joy." He was looking forward to something — he was looking forward to seeing Jesus. His mind traveled beyond the confines of the Roman jail and he saw Jesus in all of His glory, waiting to meet him with outstretched arms.

Another thought right here — when a runner runs, he runs on a well-marked-out course. He doesn't run out to either side, but he runs on the course set out for him. Likewise the Christian must run on a well-defined course. He is never to run off to the right side and play with the world and the flesh. He is never to run off to the left side to bargain with the devil. From the moment that he sees Jesus in conversion, until the moment that he sees Him face to face the Christian's course is a straight one.

And the Bible plainly tells us that the reward for the Christian race is not for speed, but for faithfulness. You and I can't run as fast as Spurgeon or Moody or Truett or Billy Graham, but we can be just as faithful as they. God takes our limitations into account and commends a two talent man in the same way that He does the five talent man. "All service ranks the same with God." It is faithfulness that counts.

Paul next says that he has "kept the faith." The doctrines of the Christian faith had been delivered supernaturally to Paul and he had never doubted the truth nor had he deviated from it. He believed that the Bible was the infallible Word of God. He believed in the virgin birth of Christ, he believed in His sinless life, he believed in His mighty miracles, he believed in His vicarious death, he believed in His victorious resurrection, he believed in His ascension and His coming again. He believed in heaven and hell and judgment. He told men everywhere that they were lost in sin and needed the cleansing blood of Christ applied to their souls. He preached repentance and faith everywhere. We need these same truths sounded out today from every pulpit and preaching platform in the world.

I heard a scientist say the other night that the ministers of today are more skeptical than the scientists. I am sure that this is true, for many ministers doubt the things that are contained in the Word of God. But the scientist, seeing so many unbelievable things coming to pass every day, no longer doubts the miracles of the Bible and the warnings of greater things to come.

Paul said that even if an angel from heaven came down and preached any other Gospel, he should be accursed. No preacher on earth has the right to stand before his people in these perilous times and preach anything else but Christ and Him crucified. He is the only hope that we have.

During World War II a doctor in a certain hospital heard a soldier saying, "Blood, blood, blood." He thought that the boy was just overcome at the sight of so much bloodshed and suffering, so he tried to divert his mind to something else. But the boy smiled and said, "I wasn't thinking of the blood upon the battlefield, I was thinking of how precious the blood of Christ is to me as I am dying." He had been taught the right kind of faith — the faith that held up in the hour of death.

In recent years we have heard the words "blood bath" being used. This world needs a blood bath all right. It needs to be washed in the blood of Calvary's Lamb.

> What can wash away my sin?
> Nothing but the blood of Jesus.
> What can make me whole again?
> Nothing but the blood of Jesus.
> Oh, precious is the flow,
> That makes me white as snow,
> No other fount I know,
> Nothing but the blood of Jesus.

Paul looks back now and what does he see? He sees a multitude of souls, saved by grace and winging their way to heaven because he did not deviate from the true faith, but because he kept that faith and gave it to them. One day you will be coming to the end of the way. It may be sooner than you expect. The casket in which you are going to lie may already be waiting for you in the local undertaker's parlor. When you lie down to die, will you be able to see anyone in your mind's eye that is in heaven or on the way to heaven because of the way that you have kept the faith? You don't have to be a preacher to keep the faith. You can keep it by your consecrated Christian living and your faithful witness to Christ.

Fifty years ago the British army in Egypt was commanded to march to a certain place by night so as not to be observed. They had to go across the desert, but they had none of our modern instruments to guide them. A young man volunteered to lead them. All night they followed him and at dawn they attacked the enemy. The victory was won, but the young man who led them was mortally wounded. He lived only a short time. When the commander came in to thank him, the young man said, "Sir, I led them straight, didn't I? I led them straight, didn't I?" The officer assured him that he had indeed led them straight.

Oh, I covet this for every Christian — that at the end of

The End of the Trail (Part Two)

the way the Great Commanding Officer might be able to say to you, "By the way you lived and served Me, you led men straight. You kept the faith."

II. Now We Think of the Crown

Paul said, "Henceforth there is laid up for me a crown of life." Paul was looking forward to seeing Christ, but evidently he knew that he would not immediately receive his crown. It was laid up for him in heaven until some other time. That time would come when he stood before the Judgment Seat. That's where the Christian receives his reward. In Corinthians Paul tells us that if our works have not been for God's glory, they will be burned up by the judgment fires. Our soul will be saved, but there will be no reward. However, if we have glorified God in our Christian works, there will be a reward waiting for us at the end of the way.

Does this mean that Paul has not yet received his full reward? Exactly. He has been with Christ all these years and that is wonderful, but the full reward is not yet his. The fruits of his labors are not yet complete. Even today the work of Paul is bringing souls to Christ all over the world. So at the judgment day, all the returns will be in — then Paul's reward will be much greater than it would have been two thousand years ago.

"Blessed are the dead which die in the Lord henceforth: Yea, saith the Spirit, that they may rest from their labours; and their works do follow them" (Revelation 14:13). What is this verse saying? It is saying that our works go on after we die. Our influence lives on. So then it can only be at the end of the way that all of our works are completed. Then when all the results have been counted up, we shall be rewarded accordingly.

For instance, I have had the privilege of writing several books of sermons. I have received letters telling me that souls were saved because of these books in places where

I have never been. Suppose that a person is saved through the reading of one of these books ten years after I am dead. The reward for that could come only after God has closed His books and counted up the score.

Now Paul tells us that this crowning is waiting, not only for him, but for all who love Christ's appearing. I would like to ask you a question — do you look forward to seeing Jesus? Are you longing for His return? If you are not a Christian, of course, you dread His coming, because it will mean nothing good for you. You need to prepare to meet God. If you are a Christian and are not living for Christ and serving Him as you should, you will be ashamed to meet Him. Oh, why don't you resolve even now that you are going to live a better life for Him, so that you, too, can look forward to His coming?

Look back into that dark Roman cell. The faithful old apostle is looking two ways. He is looking back over his life and remembering all the sufferings, persecutions and troubles. Then he is looking forward to Christ and the crown. And how does he sum it all up? How do the scales tip? I hear Him saying, "I reckon that the sufferings of this present time are not worthy to be compared with the glory which shall be revealed in us."

You may have a hard time, you may suffer persecution and ridicule and sorrow. The road of life may be rough. But I want to tell you that these things cannot compare with the glory and joy which will be yours when you see Jesus face to face. So keep up the good fight, dear Christian, run your course well, keep the faith. Do your best for Jesus, whatever happens, and the toils of the road will seem nothing when you get to the end of the way.

Christ wants everyone in the world to come to the end of the way as Paul did. He wants you to be ready for the departure time. He wants to have a crown laid up for you in heaven. Surely He is here to invite you to Him today. Can't you see Him with your heart? There are scars in

His forehead where the crown of thorns rested. There are scars in the center of both hands as He holds them out to greet you. There are scars in the insteps of both feet as He advances toward you. There is a scar in His side where the sword pierced His heart. Oh, let me introduce Him to you! He is the Son of God, the Lover of your soul, the Saviour of men. And why does He come? I can hear His answer, "I have come to wash away all of your sins. I have come to fill your heart with peace and joy. I have come to be your Best Friend in life and death. I have come to lead you along the way which ends in the city whose streets are paved with pure gold and where the ransomed hosts of glory enjoy eternal bliss!"

What is your response to this royal invitation? What will you do with Jesus?

Sermon 11

THE GREATEST VISIT EVER MADE

John 1:1-13

As we look back down the corridors of time we see that many wonderful visits have been made. In the early days of the world, when Adam and Eve were living in the Garden of Eden, God came down every evening and walked with them through that beautiful garden. That was a wonderful visit. Later on when the world was sunk in sin, God came down and visited Noah. He told Noah that He was going to destroy the world with a flood, and commanded him to build an ark to save the race. That was a wonderful visit. Then came the day when God wanted to test Abraham's love. He commanded him to take his only son, Isaac, and offer him upon the mountain as a human sacrifice. That also was a wonderful visit. After Paul was thrown to the ground on the Damascus Road, after he had heard the voice of Jesus, he was led into the city where he prayed as a blind man for three days. Then God sent Ananias to tell him what God wanted him to do. Thus began a great ministry. This was also a wonderful visit. On one of Paul's journeys, he came to Miletus and called all of the Ephesian elders to meet him there. They had a great meeting down by the seashore. He charged them to be true to Christ and the Gospel and told them good-by. Then, knowing that they would never see the preacher again, they wept and kissed him good-by. That also was a wonderful visit. When John was an old man he was banished to the Isle of Patmos for preaching the Gospel. There God pinned back the curtain of eternity, showed

The Greatest Visit Ever Made

him the future, and told him to write it down. That was a wonderful visit.

But the most wonderful, the most glorious, the most meaningful visit ever made was when God became flesh and visited this world in the form of His Son. You know all the details of that virgin birth, that sinless life, that vicarious death, that victorious resurrection and ascension. Now John speaks of that visit and how it was received in the first verses of the first chapter of John. There are four things that we see here: the Creation, the Coming, the Crime and the Converts.

I. THE CREATION

Verse three tells us that "all things were made by him; and without him was not any thing made that was made." Who was John talking about? He was talking about Jesus Christ. We say that God created all things. Yes, but He created them through His Son. Verse 1 tells that Jesus was in the beginning with God. Go back to the time when God created the world, and you find Jesus by His side. When God said, "Let there be light," Christ was there. When God said, "Let us make the sea and the dry land," Christ was there. When God said, "Let us make the animals and the fish and the fowls," Christ was there. When God said, "Let us make man in our own image," Christ was there as the agent of creation.

Now man doesn't create anything. He simply makes something out of existing material. But Christ, as the agent of creation, made everything out of nothing. He simply spoke and it came into being. Man can build a skyscraper one hundred stories high. He can build a bridge that spans a mighty river, he can build a plane that flies six hundred miles per hour. He can build a ship that sails upon the water or a submarine that runs under the water. He can make vitamins that build men up or bombs that tear them down. But in all of his building, he must use materials already here. Only God can create something out of nothing.

Jesus created the blue heavens above. Jesus created the space between the earth and the sky. Jesus scooped out the rivers and lakes and oceans and filled them with water. Jesus put the sun and the moon and the stars where they are. Jesus put the flowers in the fields and the trees in the forests. Jesus put the fish in the sea, the birds in the air, and the animals on the land. Then Jesus made His masterpiece, man, and put him down here in the world.

Yes, as the song says, "The great Creator became our Saviour." God was the source of creation, but Jesus was the instrument which brought to pass all that we see in the world. So we look back and see Jesus living with God the Father in the beginning, ages before His wonderful visit to earth.

II. THE COMING

There came a day in heaven when God decided to send His Son into the world. Why did He do that? For one reason only—He saw that men were lost and going down to hell and He wanted to provide a way of salvation for them. So God sent His Son into the world that through Him men might be saved. He came as a babe, He grew up to manhood, He went about doing good, He performed many miracles and taught the great truths of God. Finally He was crucified upon Calvary's cross. As He hung there we see God's purpose being fulfilled. Christ came not primarily as a doer of good deeds or a teacher of great truths. He came to die for sinners. "God commendeth his love toward us, in that, while we were yet sinners, Christ died for us" (Romans 5:8).

Especially at Christmas time do we hear men telling why they think Jesus came into the world. Some say that He came to bring peace to the nations. If that is so, His coming was a failure, because we have never had peace upon

The Greatest Visit Ever Made

the earth. Some say that He came to set an example of brotherly love for us, teaching us to do kind things for others. Some say that He came to establish the brotherhood of man and the Fatherhood of God upon the earth. Oh, why do men get so far away from God's Word? The greatest verse in the Bible tells us why He came, "God so loved the world, that he gave his only begotten Son, that whosoever believeth in him should not perish, but have everlasting life." That's why He came.

During the gold rush, which came to California in 1849, a Methodist preacher arrived upon the scene. He did not come seeking for gold, but for the souls of men. There was no church for him to preach in and no congregation interested in the things of God. But the people were there and he knew that they needed Christ. So on Sunday morning he would stand on a barrel and shout, "What's the news? What's the news?" Then when the crowd had gathered around he would say to them, "Thank God, I have good news for you this morning, my brothers." Then he would talk to them of Christ.

Oh, this world has received some good news over the centuries, but the greatest, grandest news ever received was the news that Christ was born, born to give the second birth, born to die that we might forever live.

Several years ago a young doctor went to China as a medical missionary. Soon he was confronted with a disease which was killing many people, and for which he knew no remedy. This disease was not listed in any medical book. There was no laboratory in China where he could do research work. So this doctor did a daring thing — he studied patient after patient and filled his notebook with a list of their symptoms. Then he filled several tubes with the germs of this disease and took a ship for America. Just before he landed in New York City he took these deadly germs into his own body and then hurried to Johns Hopkins Hospital. He presented himself as a guinea pig to the professors in the hospital. They studied the disease and found a remedy. By the grace of God this young doctor lived and carried the remedy back to China, there to save hundreds of lives.

That's a slight picture of what the coming of Jesus meant. He saw men dying in sin. And what did He do? He came and took our sin in His own body and died of the disease on the cross. That is the purpose of His coming. He came to die that we might live forever.

III. THE CRIME

This crime is listed in John 1, verse 11, "He came unto his own, and his own received him not." This is earth's blackest sin, the world's greatest crime. The men who start wars and bring sorrow and death upon millions of people are committing a crime. The man who puts the bottle to his neighbor's lips commits a crime, so says the Bible. The man who murders, who steals, who breaks the other laws of God is criminal. But here is the greatest crime — Jesus came with His hands full of blessings, holding them out to the men of His day. But they rejected Him. They turned their backs upon Him. Then they finally killed Him.

Today as you think about the crucifixion, you say, "I wouldn't have treated Him that way. I would have taken Him into my heart and home and given Him the best that I had." I wonder. I wonder. He comes to men today, even as He did then, but like the innkeeper, they have no room for Him. Yet we know who He is and what He can do for us. Those men of old didn't know these things. Surely our crime is greater than theirs.

Why don't men receive Jesus into their hearts? It is because those hearts are too full of the things of this world. Why don't they take Him into their social lives? It is because He would cramp their style. They want to do the things there which He would not approve of. Why don't they take Him into their business lives? Because then every deal would have to be as honest as the sunlight and maybe they would not make as much money. Why don't they take Him into their home lives? Often it is because the family knows one's life doesn't measure up and he would be a hypocrite if he talked there about Jesus.

Why continue to be a criminal? Why not make a new start today? Why not make room in every area of your life for Jesus? I read the other day of how one man went into another man's office and shot this man several times, killing him in cold-blooded, premeditated murder. Then I said to myself, "How foolish. Now that man knows he has no life left for himself. It's either the electric chair or life imprisonment for him." But the man who rejects Jesus Christ is the greater fool. He has nothing for himself but death and hell.

IV. THE CONVERTS

Now we come to the bright side of the picture. Verse 12 says, "As many as received him, to them gave he power to become the sons of God." It does not say as many as live good lives, nor as many as join the church, nor as many as are baptized, but as many as receive Christ. There is just one way for you to become a child of God. You must receive Jesus Christ as your Saviour.

There are many people who admire Him, there are many who believe that He is the Son of God. There are many who read about Him and many who love to hear songs and sermons about Him. But they have not received Him in their hearts and that is the one thing they must do to have eternal life. The minute you receive Him in your heart, you will want to confess Him before men. For the Bible says, "With the heart man believeth unto righteousness, and with the mouth confession is made unto salvation, for whosoever believeth on him shall not be ashamed."

And what do these become who receive Jesus? They become the sons of God. And, oh, the marvelous things that God will do for His children! He will wash away their sins. He will give them peace of heart and mind. He will walk down life's pathway with them all the way. He will be there with them in the hour of death. He will take them home to heaven at the close of life's day.

Dr. R. G. Lee won a young man and young woman to Christ. He baptized them and later married them. A year later a little baby girl came to bind their hearts closer to each other and to God in love. Then one midnight the young father called and said, "Dr. Lee, I need you. Please come to the hospital. I'm afraid that our baby is dying." Dr. Lee went over to the hospital and found that the doctors and nurses were doing all that they could for the baby. But the case was hopeless and all that he and the parents could do was stand by and watch the baby die. The preacher tried to comfort the young mother, but his words seemed to be in vain. Soon the undertaker came and wrapped the baby in a little shawl and started out the door with it. Then the mother cried out, "Oh, let me have my baby just one more night! Please, just one more night."

The husband said, "Preacher, what must I do?"

And Dr. Lee answered, "Let her have the baby just one more night." The undertaker put the child, wrapped in the beautiful shawl, into the mother's arms. The preacher went home with the young couple. He said that the mother sat there with the dead baby in her lap. She cooed and talked to the baby, but there was no light in the baby's eyes, no laughter on its lips, no warmth in the little body. Yet she had it — just one more night.

But for the children of God there is a land where there is no night, no death, no sorrow. It is a land where we shall have our loved ones, not for just a little while, but forever. I am glad that Jesus visited the world and made all of this possible. I am glad that He went to Calvary for us all, and I am glad that He can visit any open heart, bringing joy and peace and eternal life to that heart.

Sermon 12

THE VOICE OF JESUS

John 7:40-46

The human voice is a wonderful thing. Man is the only animal to whom God has given the gift of speech. With the voice a man can say to his beloved, "I love you." With his voice he can sing the praises of his God. He can make his wishes known to his fellow man. He can express his appreciation to those who have been a blessing to him. He can raise that voice in prayer to God. He can use it to preach the unsearchable riches of Christ.

Chrysostom of Constantinople was called the "Golden-Mouthed" because of his resonant voice. It was said that George Whitefield could speak certain words which would melt his audience to tears. John Wesley, when he was over seventy years of age, spoke often in the open air to audiences of thirty thousand. Spurgeon preached to congregations of two thousand people morning and night for many years. It was reported that those on the back seat could hear him perfectly and yet his voice did not seem harsh to those on the front seat.

But let us think of the voice of Jesus. It must have been rich and full and vibrant. One day He got into a boat and pushed out from the shore and spoke to the people. They could hear Him well over the sound of the lapping waves. In Revelation we read that "His voice was as the sound of many waters." But there is something more important than the sound of the voice — it is what you say with that voice. One day the Pharisees sent officers to arrest Jesus, but they came back empty-handed. When they were asked why they had not arrested Him, the officers said, "It was the way He talked. He said such wonderful things. Never did man speak as He speaks."

Jesus said many marvelous things in the long, long ago. He still says the same things today. Let us hear what He has to say even now. He is the same yesterday, today and forever, and the truths that He proclaimed two thousand years ago are just as true and appropriate today.

I. He Said, "Except Ye Repent, Ye Shall All Likewise Perish."

Jesus knows what many men are not willing to admit. They have sinned, they are lost, they can never see God and inherit eternal life until they repent of sin and turn to God through faith in Christ. You can't explain repentance without combining it with faith. These are twin doctrines. These are inseparable graces. If a man repents of his sin in the Bible way, he will exercise faith in Christ. If he exercises faith in Christ, we can know that first he has repented of his sins.

Paul connects the two when he says, "Repentance toward God and faith toward the Lord Jesus Christ." Our repentance is toward God because it is His law that has been broken. Our faith is toward Christ because He is the object of saving faith. When a man sees himself as a lost sinner, when he wants to be saved, when he wants his sin forgiven, when he wants to be counted as a child of God, when he wants to find hope for the life to come, he must repent of his sins and look up in faith to the Lord Jesus Christ. Not only is he to be sorry for his sins, but he must forsake them and turn his life over to Christ.

One night a group of seminary students heard a fire engine go by. They followed the fire engine blocks to a sanitarium which was burning down. These students went in with the firemen and helped to bring out the patients on the first two floors. Then as they stood in front of the building, they heard screams from the rear of the building. They rushed around to the back and found that four men were trapped on the third floor and were standing at the window pleading for someone to save them from the flames. Since all the ladders were being used, four firemen set up a net and then cried out to these men, "Leap down one at a time and we will save you." The first three men leaped to safety and were caught in the net. The fourth man drew back in fear. He said, "I am afraid to risk the net. Isn't there some other way?" The firemen and the students cried out, "The net is safe. Leap out and we will save you." But the man would not risk it. He turned back in the building and later they found his charred body. Listen, men without Christ are in danger of the eternal flames. There is only one way of escape. A man must repent of his sins and put his trust in Christ. This is the safe way. This is the only way. All of your goodness, your works and your gifts cannot save you. Jesus would say today as He said when He was here upon earth, "Repent of your sins and trust Me and you will be eternally saved."

"Neither is there salvation in any other; for there is none other name under heaven given among men whereby we must be saved" (Acts 4:12).

"Jesus saith unto him, I am the way, the truth, and the life; no man cometh unto the Father but by me" (John 14:6).

II. HE SAID, "THOU SHALT LOVE THE LORD THY GOD WITH ALL THY HEART, AND WITH ALL THY SOUL, AND WITH ALL THY STRENGTH, AND WITH ALL THY MIND."

Make a list of the things and the people that you love. Where do you put God? Many people put family or friends or possessions or pleasures first. But God should be at the top of the list. When He is there everything else will fall into its rightful place. "Seek ye first the kingdom of God and His righteousness; and all these things shall be added unto you."

If we love God, we will trust His Son and follow Him. If we love God, we will join His church and serve through it. If we love God, we will love lost souls and seek to win them. If we love God, we will love the Bible and live by it. If we love God, we will talk often to Him in prayer. If we love God, we will live a godly life. If we love God, we will give of our substance to His Kingdom. If we love God, we will love others for whom He died.

When Dr. F. B. Meyer was in Australia he said that he often felt like saying to his people, "If you love me, tell me so." They heard about this statement back in London, and when he reached home they had a big welcome meeting for him. A banner was stretched across the church saying, "We love you and we tell you so." Do you love God? Do you appreciate all the things He has done for you? Then tell Him so every day and live in such a way that everyone will know that you do love Him.

III. HE SAID, "COME UNTO ME, ALL YE THAT LABOUR AND ARE HEAVY LADEN, AND I WILL GIVE YOU REST."

A religion which has no comfort in it is a poor and worthless thing. We are living in a hard world. There is trouble on every side. Men's hearts are aching and breaking. They need a power stronger than themselves. They need a divine arm around them to comfort and strengthen them. What did the Bethany sisters do when they lost their brother, Lazarus? They sent for Jesus and He came and brought a blessing. He is the One we must send for when we are in sorrow and distress.

The English artist, Romney, married a fine young woman, but art was his greatest passion. Sir Joshua Reynolds told him that he had talents and could become a great artist if he were not burdened with a wife. So Romney left his wife and went to London. Soon he was highly successful and his pictures brought great sums of money. But as he grew older he became ill with no one to care for him. It was then that he went back to his faithful wife, who still loved him. She took him in and nursed him and cared for him tenderly as long as he lived. Has the world bruised you? Do you have a heavy heart? Then come back to Jesus, His arms are wide open to receive you. He is still there when all the world turns its back upon you. He will never leave you nor forsake you.

Several years ago an army colonel and his wife were faithful members of our church. But one day the doctors discovered that the wife had cancer. She didn't last very long. Just before the funeral the colonel came to look for the last time into her face. As I watched him I could see that his heart was breaking with sorrow. But in a moment he looked up and into a picture of the face of Christ. He seemed to find comfort and strength as he thought of this One who said, "Come unto me, all ye that labour and are heavy laden, and I will give you rest."

IV. HE SAID, "FOR WHAT SHALL IT PROFIT A MAN, IF HE SHALL GAIN THE WHOLE WORLD, AND LOSE HIS OWN SOUL?"

Queen Elizabeth I lay dying. She had 10,000 dresses in her wardrobe. Her kingdom spread over all the earth. But she had wasted her years in the things of this world, so she cried out, "Millions for an inch of time." At the end of the way, all that counts is our faith in Christ. If you use your life in gaining and getting, in pleasure and profit, there will be no chance for you out there.

A certain college student was a fine mathematician, but he was not a Christian. His room-mate wanted to win him to Christ. One day he handed this young man a folded piece of paper and said to him, "Here is a problem I wish you would solve." When the room-mate had left the room, the student unfolded the paper and read these words, "What shall it profit a man, if he shall gain the whole world, and lose his own soul?" He impatiently tore up the paper and threw it in the wastebasket, but he could not shake off the impression the question had raised. He found no peace until he had found Christ. Later he was called to preach and used this text for his first sermon.

I walked down a city street the other day and saw a diamond in a jewelry store window priced at $11,000.00. Many other expensive diamonds surrounded it. But the soul of one man is worth more than all the diamonds in the world. No wonder Christ was ready to die for it. A rich man died and someone asked the question, "How much did he leave?" The answer came back, "He left it all." This is true — you can't take it with you. You can buy many things here but you can't buy heaven and everlasting life. Oh, what folly for a man to spend all of his time and energy on the things of this world and then be forced to leave it all and go out into eternal night!

V. HE SAID, "LOVE YOUR ENEMIES, BLESS THEM THAT CURSE YOU, DO GOOD TO THEM THAT HATE YOU, AND PRAY FOR THEM WHICH DESPITEFULLY USE YOU AND PERSECUTE YOU."

Now this is a big order. Unless Christ dwells in your heart, you cannot love your enemies. There is only one thing that will make you love people and pray for them and do good for them after they have done evil to you. You must have the spirit of Christ Himself. I am afraid that few Christians have this spirit. They have too much of the old carnal nature in them. When someone hits them, they want to hit back. When someone curses and persecutes them, they want to kill them.

But when is the human soul strongest? Is it in some great hour when the heart is lifted up in praise to God? Is it when you perform some mighty task for the Lord? Is it when you lay some great gift upon the altar of Christ? Oh, no! The soul is strongest when it is forgiving an injury. During World War II a young American pilot was captured by the Japanese. He was persecuted and tortured for many months. After he was released by the Americans, it was a long time before he was well and strong again. But where is he now? Is he eating out his heart with hatred for those people? No, he is back in Japan, preaching the Gospel to those who tortured him. What made him do it? The only answer is that he had the spirit of Christ in his heart.

Someone has said that "hatred is self-punishment." How true this is. When you hate someone it hurts you more than it does them. It dries up all the happiness of your heart. It destroys the power of your spiritual life. Let others hate you if they must, but if someone has done you wrong, ask God to help you to forgive and forget the injury. Ask God to help you love your enemies.

VI. He Said, "Men Ought Always to Pray and Not to Faint."

A certain college president lay dying and when he was told that he had only a half hour to live, he said, "Then take me out of the bed and put me on my knees and let me spend these precious minutes in prayer." But we must not wait until we are dying. We ought to pray always.

A chaplain, who went overseas during the war, said that he asked many men the same question, "When the shells were bursting around you, and men were being killed on every side, what did you do?" And he said that everyone answered, "Oh, sir, I prayed!" Yes, it is fine to have a God who hears us in our troubles. But we are not to wait until trouble and danger come — we must pray every day. He blesses us every day, and we need to thank Him for these blessings. We sin every day and we need to ask forgiveness for these sins.

The keeper of a certain vineyard in London said that his vines bore little fruit. Then one year these same vines were full of the most luscious grapes. He began to trace the roots of the vines and he learned that they had reached out and touched the Thames River, finding there the strength and nourishment which they had never had before. When you see some great Christian, bearing fruit for the Lord, you can know this, he has learned the secret of prayer. He has sent his roots down deep and has found the strength and nourishment which only God can give.

VII. HE SAID, "GO YE THEREFORE, AND TEACH ALL NATIONS, BAPTIZING THEM IN THE NAME OF THE FATHER, AND OF THE SON, AND OF THE HOLY GHOST: TEACHING THEM TO OBSERVE ALL THINGS WHATSOEVER I HAVE COMMANDED YOU: AND, LO, I AM WITH YOU ALWAY, EVEN UNTO THE END OF THE WORLD."

Samuel Johnson said this about John Wesley, "His conversation is good, but he is never at leisure. He always has to go at a certain hour. This is very disagreeable to a man who loves to fold his legs and talk, as I do." Wesley lived ninety years. His legs were always unfolded. He was always on the go. He was always seeking souls for the Saviour. There are three great verbs in the Christian vocabulary. First, there is the verb, "Come." We are to come to Him for salvation and eternal life. Next, there is the verb, "Tarry." We are to wait until we are endued with power from on high. Third, there is the verb, "Go." We are to go with the message of Christ to the lost souls of the world.

We are soldiers of the greatest army in the world. Our Great Leader, the Lord Jesus Christ, commands us to witness everywhere for Him. God help us to be faithful to Him and to be willing to die rather than disobey Him.

VIII. He Said, "In My Father's House Are Many Mansions, If It Were Not So I Would Have Told You. I Go to Prepare a Place for You. And If I Go and Prepare a Place for You, I Will Come Again and Receive You unto Myself; that Where I Am There Ye May Be Also."

This little world isn't all. The struggle here isn't all. God has something better waiting for us. When we come to the end of the way, we need have no fear. God is just going to lift us up out of our troubles and give us a mansion beyond the blue. There will be no dark valleys when Jesus comes. There will be Someone waiting to carry us home.

A boy from a certain home started going to Sunday school and church and soon found Christ as his Saviour. His mother, who was not a Christian, had a morbid fear of death. The boy begged her to go to church, but she refused because she was afraid that the preacher would say something about death. But on Easter Sunday the boy heard the beautiful story of how Jesus rose from the dead. He hurried home with a shining face and cried out, "Mother, you need not be afraid of dying anymore. Jesus went through the grave and left a light behind Him." The mother's heart was touched. That night she heard her boy praying, "Lord, make my mother a Christian." His prayer was answered. Soon the mother went to church and came to know Christ as her Saviour. Death has no terrors for a Christian. I hear many loved ones weep as they stand beside the casket of one whom they have lost. The separation is indeed bad for them, but the one who has died in Christ is a million times better off. "Blessed are the dead which die in the Lord."

Let's go back across the centuries. We see a little band of Christians being led to the center of the coliseum in Rome. We hear the thunderous noise of the Roman crowds as they anticipate a day of bloody sport. We hear the roar of the hungry lions, eager to pounce upon their helpless prey. The little group of Christians kneels to pray. The glory of God shines upon their faces. Nero looks at them and says to his aide, "They see something which we do not see." And the aide replies, "Yes, sire, they see another world." When this hour comes for us, it need not be a dark hour. By faith we can look beyond the grave and see heaven and Jesus waiting for us.

You have heard some of the things which Jesus would say today if He were here. It makes all the difference in the world as to how you hear and heed. It also makes all the difference in the world to come. . . . Two men lived side by side. They were in business together. One was a Christian and the other was not. The Christian often pressed the claims of Christ upon his partner, but he could make no headway. These men prospered for a while, they had nice homes and good families. But when hard times came they lost everything that they had. The man who was not a Christian went home, went upstairs, and killed himself. In distress himself, he brought distress upon others. The Christian man had to give up his store and move out of his nice home. But he had something inside which kept him going. He took a job as a clerk. But he was always at church and always on the job for the Lord. His testimony in the prayer meeting was a little sweeter because of the experience he had had.

One man came down to die, wallowed in his own blood, and went out into eternity without hope. When the other man came down to die, he had a halo of glory about his head. Victory was in his voice and peace was in his heart. It pays to depend upon Jesus for this life and the life to come.